A Student's
Vocabulary for

BIBLICAL
HEBREW
AND
ARAMAIC

UPDATED EDITION

A Student's Vocabulary for

BIBLICAL HEBREW AND ARAMAIC

UPDATED EDITION

Frequency Lists with Definitions,
Pronunciation Guide, and Index

Larry A. Mitchel

ZONDERVAN

A Student's Vocabulary for Biblical Hebrew and Aramaic
Copyright © 1984, 2017 by Larry A. Mitchel

Requests for information should be addressed to:
Zondervan, *3900 Sparks Dr. SE, Grand Rapids, Michigan 49546*

ISBN 978-0-310-53387-0

Cover design: Veldheer Creative Services

Printed in the United States of America

HB 08.25.2020

To Leona Glidden Running† for whom Semitic languages are a consuming and contagious interest.

TABLE OF CONTENTS

AUTHOR'S PREFACE

Purpose of this Student's Vocabulary

In light of the availability of a number of Hebrew vocabulary lists, it is proper to ask why another such list should be put in print. The volumes that first come to mind each make a real contribution. George M. Landes's *A Student's Vocabulary of Biblical Hebrew* has an obvious advantage in its grouping of Hebrew words by root, a helpful aid in learning vocabulary. The *Hebrew Vocabularies* of J. Barton Payne present the Hebrew particles in a particularly helpful way. And the small volume by John D. W. Watts (*Lists of Words Occurring Frequently in the Hebrew Bible*), which like Payne's is based on William Rainey Harper's *Hebrew Vocabularies* (published in 1890), presents Hebrew vocabulary down to twenty-five occurrences in a very compact form.

However, in my experience in teaching Biblical Hebrew on the undergraduate level, I have felt that each of the above excellent works have presented two fundamental problems for entry-level Hebrew students: (1) each volume incorporates a number of separate lists, requiring reference to various parts of the book in order to find all Hebrew words of a given frequency; and (2) the lists themselves are apparently set by somewhat arbitrary word-freqency limits, resulting in lists of greatly variable length. The present work seeks to remedy both of those basic problems.

The lexicon of Old Testament Hebrew contains some 10,000 words in all. Of these, approximately 740 occur fifty times or more. A full 490 occur as *hapax legomena* by Harold R. Cohen's definition (pp. xv, 6–7; see vol. in Select Bibliography). Many more words in the MT occur only once, though other occurrences of that same Hebrew root may also appear.

The Aramaic lexicon consists of approximately 650 words. Since the amount of Aramaic text in the Old Testament is so much less than that of Hebrew text, the number of occurrences of Aramaic words is lower.

For the Hebrew vocabulary sections (Sections 1–5) an attempt has been made to include every word that occurs ten times or more. The one exception to this inclusive statement has to do with proper nouns: only those personal and place names that are used fifty times or more are included. The primary reason for including proper nouns at all is that while some Hebrew place names and personal names are reasonably transparent to students familiar with the Old Testament in English translation, many are rather opaque. This is the case because the English transliteration that the student knows often reflects Greek forms more than the original Hebrew name. For examples of the latter, see "Isaac" (Section 3.F) or "Solomon" (2.C).

A section containing Hebrew words occurring less than ten times was prepared for this project. Simply for considerations of length it has not been included in this volume. (It was twice as long as Sections 1–4, both in number of entries and estimated page length!) Most Hebrew students would probably find little use for this section of Hebrew vocabulary.

In the case of Aramaic vocabulary (Section 6), the effort has been made to include every Aramaic word, except for proper nouns. (No personal or place names have been included, except for a few that occur more than fifty times in Aramaic and Hebrew and thus are listed in Sections 1–4 with a note regarding the number of occurrences in Aramaic.)

A glance at the Table of Contents and the first few vocabulary lists should be enough to clarify the arrangement of this volume. Instead of juggling two or three (or more) different frequency lists, all words of a given frequency range have been gathered into one list. By learning one list (or series of lists) — not two or three — a student can master all Hebrew (or Aramaic) words in that frequency range. Vocabulary learning effort can thus be better focused.

Furthermore, instead of setting arbitrary frequency ranges, this *Student's Vocabulary* has had as its priority the production of consistently short, manageable lists. In general, this means lists not in excess of thirty words. This ideal holds true until sheer numbers of words of identical frequency make smaller lists impossible, short of artificially breaking up longer lists alphabetically. (You can't have words that occur between 1.5 and 1.2 times in the MT!)

By these two devices then, combining all MT vocabulary into one sequence of lists containing less and less frequently occurring words, and adjusting frequency ranges to keep lists reasonably short, this *Student's Vocabulary* has sought to meet the pedagogical shortcomings of other available Hebrew vocabularies.

Resources for the Preparation of *A Student's Vocabulary*

A number of reference works have been used in the determination of word frequencies. Trial lists were prepared based on frequencies given by Landes and Payne. However, all the words included in this vocabulary have been independently checked — except where the number of occurrences obviously exceed 5000 — by an actual count. The primary reference works have been the concordances by Lisowsky and Mandelkern. Additionally, occasional reference has been made to Wigram's *Englishman's Hebrew and Chaldee Concordance*. Consult the Select Bibliography for publication details.

Acknowledgments

Without the help and encouragement of a large number of people this volume would not have been produced. In particular I think of two of my students at Pacific Union College, Larry Errett and Cathemae Cecchin. Larry Errett, an able linguist, did some of the earliest work on word counts, especially in the highest frequencies. And Cathe Cecchin, who worked as my secretary for three years during her undergraduate study, has nearly single-handedly accomplished the staggering task of entering encoded text destined to be translated by computer into printed and pointed Hebrew script and (at the cost of even more effort) phonetic spellings.

W. Larry Richards, Religion Department chairman during the more critical stages of research for this volume, provided much-needed encouragement, but also the sorts of scheduling concessions without which this entire project might well have foundered. Small academic institutions seldom have adequate research-support resources. However, the administration of Pacific Union College has been most helpful and cooperative, supplying both the funds for student assistants and the resources and expertise of the college computer facility.

For computer aid and expertise, Harold E. Hunt and Bernard Maron of Autographics, Inc., in Monterey Park, California, richly deserve praise. It was their work that helped turn a concept into reality, and this even though all too often my idea of how to reach reality represented rather different ways of doing things. And here at Pacific Union College, our work of data entry was made immeasurably easier, and therefore more accurate and less time consuming, by the efforts of Dr. Gilbert Muth, chairman of the Biology Department, a man who writes elegant computer programs that work (no mean feat!).

And finally, to my wife Carola, and to Carmie and Jason, I owe a large debt for constant support and understanding. Work on this project has consumed time that would have otherwise been theirs.

While every reasonable effort has been made to reduce errors to an absolute minimum, it is virtually certain a few such will remain. I would welcome any notices for corrections or improvements. Send these either directly to me or to the publisher.

Learning Hebrew vocabulary requires a lot of time and effort. I hope this volume will help both instructors and students of Biblical Hebrew and Aramaic to make the most efficient use possible of their vocabulary study time.

Larry A. Mitchel
Pacific Union College, Angwin, California 94508
December 1983

PUBLISHER'S PREFACE TO UPDATED EDITION

Mitchel's *A Student's Vocabulary for Biblical Hebrew and Aramaic* has been a standard and accessible resource for Biblical Hebrew and Aramaic language acquisition for the past few decades. For this reason Zondervan Academic saw fit to create an updated edition. The primary revision made to the 1984 edition of this volume was stylistic. The interior now follows closely *The SBL Handbook of Style Second Edition* and where the SBL styleguide fell silent or was inconsistent, easy-to-use conventions were adopted. The Select Bibliography listed in the front matter of the 1984 publication has also been updated and expanded to reflect current scholarship and language studies. Likewise, Mitchel's brief explanations in the How to Use section have been revised and updated.

The 1984 manuscript existed in an unworkable file, boasting non-Unicode fonts, and so was necessarily rekeyed. This tedious work was done by Wendy Widder. Her careful attention to detail has made my own work on this project that much more enjoyable. In the process of preparing the updated edition, care was taken to recheck and update definitions where necessary and to confirm Mitchel's frequency lists. Minimal updates needed to be made—a testimony to his initial work.

Other than the aforementioned revisions, Mitchel's primary format of listing vocabulary has been maintained. After all, it's the accessibility and ease of this volume that has placed it as an essential resource for so long. My hope is that the stylistic changes and updates here will secure his little orangey book as an important resource for many years to come.

Nancy Erickson, PhD
Senior Editor, Zondervan Academic
December 2016

HOW TO USE THIS *STUDENT'S VOCABULARY*

General Orientation

The purpose of vocabulary study is to learn the correct spelling, pronunciation, and meaning of a set of new (foreign or native) words. Since correct pronunciation of Hebrew words is an integral part of effective vocabulary learning, the student should from the beginning take seriously the matter of consonant and vowel values in Hebrew. For convenience, a chart detailing the Hebrew Alphabet, Transliteration, and Pronunciation has been provided for reference (see p. 24). However, these letters and sounds will simply have to be committed to memory before efficient study of Hebrew vocabulary can begin.

Beyond the phonetic value, or transliteration, of the Hebrew consonants and vowels themselves, Hebrew pronunciation is also determined by several other interrelated factors:

1. *Syllable division.* Hebrew syllables may be either open (consisting of a consonant followed by a vowel) or closed (a consonant, a vowel, and a consonant—in that order). For the rules governing the use of long or short vowels in a Hebrew word, the student should consult his/her grammar.

2. *Use of* shewa. Pronunciation of Hebrew words also depends upon a determination as to whether the *shewa* is vocal (stands under the opening consonant of a syllable) or silent (under the closing consonant of a syllable).

3. *Accent.* The placement of the stress in a Hebrew word can materially affect its pronunciation. This is especially obvious when the form of a word changes, for example in the formation of a plural or the addition of suffixes. In this vocabulary, accent marks are only used for multi-syllable Hebrew words that are stressed on other than the final syllable. The mark ˋis used.

4. *Furtive patach.* Some Hebrew words that end in ח and ע will take

a *patach* beneath the consonant. This is called a *furtive patach* and must be pronounced *before* the consonant. The common practice observed herein is not to show a syllable division in transliteration for furtive *patach*. Rather, the Hebrew forms show the accent mark (i.e., רָקִיעַ, *rā/qîaʿ*).

Because of these and other variables, it was decided to include in this vocabulary a transliteration of each form presented. In cases where more than one Semitic form is involved, transliterations are given in the same order as the Hebrew (or Aramaic) words. Syllable divisions and stress accents are also indicated.

Beyond proper spelling and pronunciation, the student needs to learn the meaning of the Hebrew words he/she is studying. The definitions that have been provided in this volume have been chosen in consultation with standard Hebrew lexicons (particularly William L. Holladay's *A Concise Hebrew and Aramaic Lexicon of the Old Testament.*) These meanings are in no sense full and exhaustive. For the meanings of nouns in various contexts, or of verbs in different contexts or in derived stems, the student must consult a trustworthy dictionary or lexicon. See the Select Bibliography for a number of helpful and reliable lexicons and dictionaries. Individual language teachers may wish for whatever reason to supplement or emphasize (and even in some cases supplant) given definitions. But in general the meanings given for the Hebrew words in this vocabulary have been chosen with the beginning student in mind and provide base meanings that will serve those needs.

This *Student's Vocabulary* can be used to great advantage along with *A Reader's Hebrew-English Lexicon of the Old Testament* by Armstrong, Busby, and Carr. By simply learning the Hebrew vocabulary down to fifty occurrences, about 739 words in all, a student should be able to read plain Hebrew text by following along in the appropriate section of the *Reader's Hebrew-English Lexicon* and referring there for all forms which occur less than fifty times (assuming a minimum knowledge of grammar and syntax).

Sample Entry and Explanation

Perhaps the best way to explain how the individual vocabulary entries in this volume are presented is to give examples and provide some detailed explanations. The following entries are in no way complete and exhaustive, but what they do not contain can be easily described.

*[1]בָּקַשׁ (Pi)[2] seek[3] [bā/qʹašʹ]][4]   (II)[6] אֵת (prep.)[2] with, beside
225[5]   [ʹēt] 5000[5]

[1] *Hebrew/Aramaic Word(s)*. An attempt has been made to use forms and spellings that are favored today. In making such choices, personal judgments are inevitable. Not all decisions may seem to every trained reader to be the best ones. Hopefully no decision will mislead the beginning student. One such judgment relates to Hebrew and Aramaic words spelled with a long "o." In very many cases the word appears in the MT spelled with both *holem* (˙, ō) and with full *holem* (ֹו, ô). This vocabulary has not achieved consistency on the matter: if you cannot find a word under one spelling, try the alternate spelling before giving up! (The same goes for vocalic spellings with and without *yod*.)

a. *Verbs*. Unpronounceable words are more difficult to learn—at least if the ear helps at all in vocabulary study. For this reason all verb roots have been provided with vowels. In the case of verbs that only occur in non-*qal* stems (and are thus left unpointed in most lexicons), this *Student's Vocabulary* gives to the root those vowels that pertain to the (missing) *qal* form. Since this form is hypothetical, an asterisk (*) is placed after the entry. This practice has also been observed for the so-called biconsonantal verbs (verbs with a *yod* or *waw* in the second position), even though the verb may in fact appear in just that form. (This has been done because there is often uncertainty, and some disagreement, regarding the appropriate vowel.) Furthermore, in many cases the verb, though used in the *qal*, may not occur in the third masculine singular even though the asterisk is missing.

b. *Nouns, Adjectives, Prepositions*. An asterisk after these forms signals that while this is the dictionary form of the word, for one reason or another the word never appears just this way in the MT. (As a rule, simple changes in form, such as the addition of a suffixed pronoun or the construct state have not been listed in this vocabulary with an asterisk.) An explanation of the reason for the asterisk is provided in the definition section.

c. *General Comments.* The names of ancient Near Eastern countries and their respective gentilic (people-naming) nouns have been combined in single entries and listed according to total number of occurrences.

Numerals have also been gathered into single entries, corresponding words for multiples of ten (twenty, thirty, etc.) being given under the Hebrew word for that number. Numbers from three to ten are identified by the gender of the form. (In that range Hebrew uses feminine numerals for masculine nouns, and vice versa — a device called chiastic concord in some grammars.)

Occasionally, particularly for words of low frequency, there is considerable uncertainty even regarding a hypothetical vowel-point assignment. In such cases the Semitic word is followed by a question mark in parentheses (?).

2 *Grammar/Morphology.* Information of importance or convenience about a word's part of speech, derived stem, or person/gender/number is given in abbreviated form preceding the definitions. The meaning of these abbreviations may be found in the list of Abbreviations and Symbols.

In the case of verbs that do not appear in the MT in the *qal* stem, the Hebrew form appears in this vocabulary with an asterisk (as mentioned above). The note in parentheses at the beginning of the definition section then indicates the most commonly used (or the simplest) derived stem in which that verb does occur.

In the case of nouns, adjectives, prepositions, and such, the note in parentheses identifies the part of speech and/or the reason why the asterisk has been used.

3 *Word Meaning.* Levels of difference in the meanings for a given word have been indicated by separating punctuation marks: a comma divides words which are more or less synonymous whereas a semicolon sets off extended meanings or rather different definitions. Roman numerals in parentheses refer to one of two or more roots with an identical spelling

in Hebrew/Aramaic. These designations follow Holladay's lexicon. Definitions are of the Semitic word as given (not, for example, in plural, even if the asterisk means that this word only occurs in the plural form).

Cross references in the vocabulary are identified by Section number and Subsection letter (i.e., cf. 1.D).

[4] *Transliteration.* As an aid to self-study, each entry includes a phonetic spelling. Beginning students should find this feature to be helpful as they begin to learn Semitic vocabulary since it will aid in correct pronunciation of Hebrew/Aramaic words thus enlisting the ear as well in vocabulary learning. It will be necessary to learn the proper values for each symbol from the chart detailing the Hebrew Alphabet, Transliteration, and Prounciation. Syllables are separated by slashes (/). Accented syllables have been indicated by ′, except for mono-syllabic words.

[5] *Number of Occurrences.* Counts for Hebrew words are inclusive and for that reason somewhat overlapping. This means, for example, that a *qal* active participle may be counted among the occurrences of the verb and counted again when used as a noun. Such situations are limited primarily to words which occur often enough as substantives to justify also treating them as a vocabulary entry in their own right. In the case of *qal* participles, only those occurring ten times or more have been listed in their own entries.

Commonly, word counts include forms of the word that have been prefixed (by the article or prepositions), pluralized, and/or suffixed (by pronouns). In some situations in which such forms have become standardized (and are numerous), prefixed or suffixed forms are listed in separate entries. For verbs, the indicated count includes not only the implied or indicated verbal stems (*qal, hiphil,* etc.), but all stems in which that verb appears.

Word counts from Lisowsky's concordance include *qere* readings as well as normal occurrences. With proper nouns (where given), all occurrences of a given name are included, even though in many cases more than one referent is intended.

In cases where Mandelkern and Lisowsky disagree as to number of occurrences, the general practice has been to enter the higher of the counts, unless further work (sometimes including entry-by-entry comparisons) has made it clear the lower number is to be preferred.

Words identified as occurring 5000 times occur *more* than 5000 times. No attempt has been made to precisely establish the occurrences of these twelve Hebrew words.

6 *Root Number.* As indicated earlier, root designations follow Holladay's lexicon. In some cases several roots have been combined, for one reason or another, into one entry. In such situations the meanings of the various roots have been designated within the definition section.

Suggestions for Using This *Student's Vocabulary*

As has been widely acknowledged, learning vocabulary and retaining it are probably the most challenging aspects of learning Hebrew or Aramaic. In my experience the principle reason for this fact is that, in contrast to New Testament Greek, Old Testament Hebrew and Aramaic have virtually no cognate words in English. This requires much more rote memorization or the formation of idiosyncratic memory devices. While each student must determine what works best for vocabulary study, here are a few commonsense suggestions.

1. *Flash cards.* While not all language students use them, homemade flash cards provide several advantages in vocabulary learning. First, you must go through the motions of writing the foreign word and its definition. Second, punched and carded on a ring holder, flash cards are very transportable for study at odd times and in many places. Third, flash cards can be (and probably should be) rearranged as you learn words, so that less time is spent on words that only need to be reviewed while more effort is concentrated on new or recalcitrant forms.

2. *Oral repetition.* Repeating Hebrew and Aramaic words and their meanings out loud over and over (correctly!) introduces two critical factors into your vocabulary learning—pronunciation and hearing.

3. *Repeated writing.* Used alone and in connection with oral repetition, repeated writing of Old Testament vocabulary helps to establish a memory pattern.

Given the descending-frequency scheme with which this volume is prepared, a student can develop a Hebrew or Aramaic vocabulary as far as is necessary or desired (within the limits of this vocabulary volume). Within the ranges covered herein, by using the Indices and referring to the appropriate Section/Subsection location, the number of times a given word occurs in the Old Testament can be determined.

SELECT BIBLIOGRAPHY

Armstrong, Terry A., Douglas S. Busby, and Cyril F. Carr. *A Reader's Hebrew-English Lexicon of the Old Testament*. Grand Rapids: Zondervan, 1989.

Brown, Francis, S. R. Driver, and Charles A. Briggs. *A Hebrew and English Lexicon of the Old Testament*. Rev. ed. Peabody, MA: Hendrickson, 1996.

Clines, D. J. A., P. R. Davies, and J. W. Rogerson, eds. *The Dictionary of Classical Hebrew*. 5 vols. Sheffield: Sheffield Academic, 1993–2001.

Cohen, Harold R. (Chaim). *Biblical Hapax Legomena in the Light of Akkadian and Ugaritic*. SBL Dissertation Series, 37. Missoula: Scholars Press, 1978.

Davidson, B. *The Analytical Hebrew and Chaldee Lexicon*. London: Samuel Baster and Sons, 1956.

Even-Shoshan, Abraham, ed. *A New Concordance of the Old Testament: Thesaurus of the Language of the Bible, Hebrew and Aramaic, Roots, Words, Proper Names, Phrases, and Synonyms*. Jerusalem: Kiryat Sefer, 1989.

Fohrer, Georg. *Hebrew and Aramaic Dictionary of the Old Testament*. Translated by W. Johnstone. London: SCM, 2012.

Gesenius, W., E. Kautzsch, and A. E. Cowley, eds. *Gesenius' Hebrew Grammar*. Oxford: Clarendon Press, 1910.

Holladay, William L. *A Concise Hebrew and Aramaic Lexicon of the Old Testament*. Grand Rapids: Eerdmans, 1972.

Koehler, Ludwig, Walter Baumgartner, and Johann J. Stamm. *The Hebrew and Aramaic Lexicon of the Old Testament*. Translated and edited under the supervision of Mervyn E. J. Richardson. Study Edition. 2 vols. Leiden: Brill, 2001.

Lambdin, Thomas. *Introduction to Biblical Hebrew*. New York: Scribner's, 1971.

Landes, George M. *Building Your Biblical Hebrew Vocabulary: Learning Words by Frequency and Cognate.* 2nd ed. Atlanta: Society for Biblical Literature, 2001.

Lisowsky, Gerhard. *Konkordanz zum Hebräischen alten Testament.* 3rd rev. ed. Peabody, MA: Hendrickson, 2010.

Mandelkern, Solomon. *Veteris Testamenti Concordantiae Hebraicae atque Chaldaicae.* Tel Aviv: Schoken, 1986.

Owens, John Joseph. *Analytical Key to the Old Testament.* 4 vols. Grand Rapids: Baker Academic, 1992.

Payne, J. Barton. *Hebrew Vocabularies Based on Harper's Hebrew Vocabularies.* Grand Rapids: Baker, 1984.

Pleins, David J. *Biblical Hebrew Vocabulary by Conceptual Categories: A Student's Guide to Nouns in the Old Testament.* Grand Rapids: Zondervan, forthcoming 2017.

Pratico, Gary D. and Miles V. Van Pelt. *Basics of Biblical Hebrew: Grammar.* 2nd ed. Grand Rapids: Zondervan, 2007.

Pratico, Gary D. and Miles V. Van Pelt. *Biblical Hebrew: A Compact Guide.* Grand Rapids: Zondervan, 2012.

Pratico, Gary D. and Miles V. Van Pelt. *The Vocabulary Guide to Biblical Hebrew.* Grand Rapids: Zondervan, 2003.

Watts, John D. W. *Lists of Words Occurring Frequently in the Hebrew Bible.* 2nd ed. Eugene, OR: Wipf & Stock, 2008.

Wigram, George V. *The New Englishman's Hebrew-Aramaic Concordance.* Peabody, MA: Hendrickson, 1843.

Young, Robert. *Analytical Concordance to the Bible.* Peabody, MA: Hendrickson, 1984.

HEBREW ALPHABET, TRANSLITERATION, AND PRONUNCIATION

Consonants		Transliteration	Pronunciation
א	alef	ʾ	(glottal stop — none)
ב	bet	b	b as in best
ב		b	v as in vest
ג	gimel	g	g as in give
ג		ḡ	throaty gh
ד	dalet	d	d as in day
ד		d	th as in the
ה	he	h	h as in hay
ו	waw	w	w as in well
ז	zayin	z	z as in zero
ח	ḥet	ḥ	ch as in Bach
ט	tet	ṭ	t as in time
י	yod	y	y as in yes
כ	kaf	k	k as in key
כ		k	ch as in Bach
ך	(final kaf)	k	ch as in Bach
ל	lamed	l	l as in look
מ	mem	m	m as in more
ם	(final mem)	m	m as in more
נ	nun	n	n as in now
ן	(final nun)	n	n as in now
ס	samek	s	s as in say
ע	ayin	ʿ	(glottal stop — none)
פ	pe	p	p as in pay
פ		p̄	f as in face
ף	(final pe)	p̄	f as in face
צ	tsade	ṣ	ts as in sits
ץ	(final tsade)	ṣ	ts as in sits
ק	qof	q	harder than c in cool
ר	resh	r	r as in ran
שׂ	sin	ś	s as in say

שׁ	shin	š	sh as in show
תּ	taw	t	t as in try
ת		t	th as in thin

Vowels and Dipthongs	Transliteration	Pronunciation
_ pataḥ	a	a as in that
_ furtive pataḥ	a	a as in account
ָ qamets	ā	a as in father
הָ final qamets he	â	a as in father
יָ 3ms suffix	āyw	ow as in brow
ֶ segol	e	e as in let
ֵ tsere	ē	ey as in they
ֵי tsere yod	ê	ey as in they
ֶי segol yod	ey	ey as in they
ִ short ḥireq	i	i as in pin
ִ long ḥireq	ī	i as in bit
ִי ḥireq yod	î	i as in machine
ָ qamets ḥatuf	o	o as in top
ֹ ḥolem	ō	o as in note
וֹ full ḥolem	ô	o as in note
ֻ short qibbuts	u	u as in bull
ֻ long qibbuts	ū	u as in bull
וּ shureq	û	u as in flute
ֳ ḥatef qamets	ŏ	a as in about
ֲ ḥatef pataḥ	ă	a as in about
ֱ ḥatef segol	ĕ	a as in about
ְ vocal shewa	ə	a as in about
וַ	aw	ow as in prow
וָ	āw	ow as in how
יַ	ai	ay as in say
יָ	āi	i as in sigh
יֵ ,וֹ ,יֵ	ēw, êw	av as in save
יוִ	îw	ue as in hue
יֹ, יֹ	ôy, ōy	oy as in toy
וּי	ûy	uey as in gluey

ABBREVIATIONS AND SYMBOLS

A	*aphel*	fract.	fractional (number)
abs.	absolute	gent.	gentilic (noun)
acc.	accusative	Ha	*haphel*
act.	active	Heb.	Hebrew
adj.	adjective	Hi	*hiphil*
adv.	adverb	Hisht	*hishtaphal*
advs.	adversative (conjunction)	Hist	*histaphal*
alw.	always	Hith	*hithpael* (Heb.); *hithpeel*
Aram.	Aramaic		(Aram.)
art.	article	Hithpa	*hithpaal*
c.	common (gender)	Hithpal	*hithpalpel*
cf.	compare, see also; see	Hithpol	*hithpolel*
	instead	Ho	*hophal*
cj.	conjecture; conjectural	idiom.	idiom; idiomatic
coll.	collective		expression
comp.	comparison; comparative	imprec.	imprecative
conj.	conjunction	impv.	imperative
cons.	consonant	inf.	infinitive
const.	construct	interj.	interjection
corr.	corruption, textual	interr.	interrogative
ctxt.	context(ual); in context	intrans.	intransitive
def.	definite	irr.	irregular
dem.	demonstrative	Ith	*ithpeel*
den.	denominative	Ithpa	*ithpaal*
ditt.	dittography	Ithp	*ithpœl*
d.	dual	K	*ketiv* (what is written in
emph.	emphatic		MT)
ext.	by extension; extended	m.	masculine
	meaning	MT	Masoretic Text
f.	feminine	met.	metaphor(ically)

n.	noun	prep.	preposition
neg.	negative	prob.	probable
Ni	*niphal*	ptc.	participle
ord.	ordinal (number)	Pu	*pual*
Pa	*pael*	Pul	*pulal*
part.	particle	Q	*qere* (what should be
pass.	passive		read in MT)
pers.	person(al)	rel.	relative
Pe	*peal*	s.	singular
Pi	*piel*	Sha	*shapel*
Pil	*pilel*	stat.	stative
Pilp	*pilpel*	temp.	temporal
pl.	plural	trad.	traditional(ly)
Po	*pœl*	trans.	transitive
poet.	poetic; in poetry	unc.	uncertain
Pol	*polel, polal*	unex.	unexplained
poss.	possible	v.	verb
pron.	pronoun	voc.	vocative
pred.	predicate	wp.	word play
pref.	prefix(ed)		

*	hypothetical form (as such does not occur in MT)
!	indicates half-open syllable
?	indicates uncertainty regarding definition
(?)	indicates uncertainty regarding Semitic vowel(s)
†	indicates Aramaic cognate spelled like a Hebrew word
‡	indicates Aramaic cognate with different vowels from Hebrew
§	indicates Aramaic cognate spelled differently but recognizably

SECTION 1: HEBREW WORDS OCCURRING MORE THAN 500 TIMES (106)

A. Words Occurring More Than 2200 Times (25)

אֶל (prep.) unto, toward ['el] 5000

אֱלֹהִים (II) God ['ĕlō/hî'm] 2706

אָמַר (I) say ['ā/ma'r] 5000

אֶרֶץ earth ['e'/reṣ] 2498

אֲשֶׁר (rel. pron.) who, which, that ['ăše'r] 5000

אֵת (I) (acc. part.; def. object marker; not translated) ['ēt] 5000

אֵת (II) (prep.) with, beside ['ēt] 5000

בְּ (pref. prep.) in 5000

בּוֹא go in, enter, come [bô'] 2530

בֵּן (I) son [bēn] 4887

הַ (pref. def. art.) the (with dagesh in following cons.) 5000

הֲ (pref. interr. part.) 5000

הָיָה be, happen, become [hā/yá'] 3514

וְ (pref. conj.) and, also, even 5000

יהוה (full; short form) The Lord [K "Yahweh"?; Q 'ădō/na'i; yâ'] 5766

יוֹם (I) day [yôm] 2241

יִשְׂרָאֵל Israel [yiś/rā/'ēl] 2513

כְּ (pref. prep.) as, like 5000

כִּי (II) (conj.) because, for, that, when, but; indeed, truly [kî] 4395

כֹּל, כּוֹל all, every [kōl, kôl] 5000

לְ (pref. prep.) to, toward (I); (voc.) Do! Yes! (II) 5000

לֹא (neg.) no, not [lō'] 4973

מֶלֶךְ (I) king [me'/lek] 2522

עַל (II) (prep.) on, upon, against, over ['al] 4898

עָשָׂה do, make; (Pi) press, squeeze (II?) ['ā/śá'] 2573

B. Words Occurring between 2199 and 1000 Times (27)

אָב father ['ab] 1568

אִישׁ; אֲנָשִׁים (I) (s.; pl.) man ['îš; 'ănā/ší'm] 2149

אִם (conj.) if, then ['im] 1046

אֲנִי; אָנֹכִי (pers. pron. c.) I [ʾănî; ʾā/nō/kíʾ] 1316

בַּיִת (I) house [baʹyit] 2039

דָּבַר (II)* (Pi) speak [dā/baʹrᵉ] 1130

דָּבָר word, thing, matter [dā/bāʹr] 1426

דָּוִד David [dā/wíd] 1031

הוּא (pers. pron.) he [hûʾ] 1533

הָלַךְ go, walk [hā/laʹk] 1504

הֵמָּה; הֵנָּה (pers. pron. pl. m.; f.) they [hēʹm/mâ; hēʹn/nâ] 1553

הִנֵּה (dem. interj.) behold! lo! (cf. I הֵן, 3.G) [hin/nēʹh] 1037

זֶה; זֹאת (dem. pron. s. m.; f.) this [zeh; zōʾt] 1752

יָד hand [yād] 1580

יָצָא go (come) out, go (come) forth [yā/ṣāʹʾ] 1055

יָשַׁב sit, dwell, inhabit [yā/šaʹb] 1078

לִפְנֵי (prep.) before [lip̄/nēʹ] 1099

מִן (prep.) from, out of, part of, because of; (comp.) than [min] 1279

נָתַן give [nā/taʹn] 1994

עַד (II) (prep.) to, unto, as far as (spacial); until, while (temp.) [ʿad] 1246

עִיר; עָרִים (I) (f.; irr. pl.) city [ʿîr; ʿā/ríʹm] 1080

עַם (II) people [ʿam] 1827

עִם (prep.) with [ʿim] 1076

פָּנִים face [pā/níʹm] 2120

רָאָה see [rā/ʾâʹ] 1294

שׁוּב* turn, return [šûbᵉ] 1055

שָׁמַע hear, give ear to, obey [šā/maʹʿ] 1136

C. Words Occurring from 999 Times to 730 Times (28)

אָדוֹן; אֲדֹנָי lord, master; the Lord [ʾā/dôʹn; ʾădō/nāʹî] 770

אֶחָד; אַחַת (s. m.; f.) one [ʾe/ḥāʹd; ʾaḥ/ḥat] 959

אַיִן; אֵין (I) (abs.; const.) there is/ are not (non-existence) [ʾaʹ/yin; ʾên] 773

אָכַל eat, devour [ʾā/kaʹl] 795

אַל (I) no, not [ʾal] 738

אֵלֶּה (dem. pron.; c. pl.) these [ʾēl/leh] 738

אִשָּׁה; נָשִׁים (s.; irr. pl.) woman [ʾiš/ šāʹ; nā/šíʹm] 779

אַתָּה; אַתְּ (s. m.; f.) you [ʾat/tâʹ; ʾat] 893

גַּם (adv., conj.) also, indeed [gam] 812

יָדַע know, notice [yā/daʿ]
924

יְהוּדָה; יְהוּדִי (I) Judah; (gent. adj., n.)
Judean, Judahite [yəhû/
dá; yəhû/dî] 889

כֹּהֵן priest [kō/hēn] 749

לֵב; לֵבָב heart [lēb; lē/bāb] 844

לָקַח take [lā/qáḥ] 964

מָה, מֶה, מַה (interr. pron.) what?
how? [mâ, meh, mah]
760

מוּת* die [mût] 737

מֹשֶׁה Moses [mō/šeʾh] 763

נֶפֶשׁ life, self; throat [ne/
pēš] 753

עֶבֶד (I) servant [ʿe/bed] 800

עַיִן eye; fountain [ʿá/yin]
867

עָלָה go up [ʿā/lá] 879

עֶשֶׂר; עֶשְׂרִים (s. m.; c. pl.) ten (plus
num = 11–19); twenty
[ʿā/śá r; ʿeś/rî m] 819

קָרָא (I) call, meet; give a name
to; read (aloud) [qā/
rā] 730

שָׁלַח stretch out, let go, send
[šā/laḥ] 839

שָׁם (adv.) there [šām] 817

שֵׁם (I) name [šēm] 862

שָׁנָה year [šā/ná] 871

שְׁנַיִם; שְׁתַּיִם (d. m.; f.) two [šəna/
yim; šəta/yim] 739

D. Words Occurring between 729 and 500 Times (26)

אָדָם (I) man [ʾā/dā m] 553

אָח (II) brother [ʾāḥ] 626

אַחַר behind, after [ʾa!/ḥar]
713

בַּת (I) daughter [bat] 582

גָּדוֹל (adj.) great [gā/dó l]
525

גּוֹי people, nation [gôy]
545

דֶּרֶךְ way, road, journey;
(ext.) custom [de/rek]
698

הִיא (pers. pron.) she [hî]
541

הַר mountain, range [har]
554

טוֹב (I) (v.) be good; (adj.)
good; (n.) goodness
[ṭôb] 612

יְרוּשָׁלֵַם (Q) Jerusalem (26x
Aram.) [yərû/šā/la/im]
667

כַּאֲשֶׁר (conj.) as [ka!/ʾăšer]
504

כֹּה (adv.) thus, so [kōh]
554

כֵּן (adv., adj., n.) rightly,
upright, right (I); (adv.)
thus, so (II) [kēn] 707

מֵאָה (I) hundred; (d.) two
hundred [mē/ʾá] 577

מַיִם water [ma/yim] 574

מִצְרַיִם; מִצְרִי Egypt; (gent.) Egyptian [miṣ/ra'/yim; miṣ/ri'] 708

נָכָה* (Ni) be hit; (Hi) smite [nā/ká'ʰ] 504

נָשָׂא lift up, bear, carry [nā/śā'ʰ] 651

עָבַר (I) pass over, transgress [ʿā/ba'r] 539

עָמַד stand [ʿā/ma'd] 519

קוּם* rise, stand [qûmᵉ] 624

רֹאשׁ (I) head [rō'š] 593

רַע, רַע; רָעָה (s. m.; f.; adj., n.) evil [rā', ra'; rā/ʿá'] 661

שִׂים* (I) set, place [śîmᵉ] 584

שָׁלֹשׁ, שְׁלֹשָׁה; שְׁלֹשִׁים (s. m., f.; pl.) three; thirty [šā/lō'š, šəlō/šá'; šəlō/ší'm] 586

2.A

SECTION 2: HEBREW WORDS OCCURRING BETWEEN 500 AND 200 TIMES (136)

A. Words Occurring between 500 and 400 Times (28)

אֶלֶף thousand (II?); tribe, clan (III?) [ʾeʹ/lep] 494

אַרְבַּע, אַרְבָּעָה; (s. m., f.; pl.) four; forty אַרְבָּעִים(I) [ʾar/baʻ, ʾar/bā/ʻâ; ʾar/bā/ʻîʹm] 444

בְּתוֹךְ Cf. תָּוֶךְ

חָמֵשׁ, חֲמִשָּׁה; (s. m. f.; pl.) five; fifty חֲמִשִּׁים [ḥā/mēʹš, ḥămiš/šâʹ; ḥămiš/šîʹm] 478

חֶרֶב sword [ḥeʹ/reb] 407

יָלַד bring forth, bear [yā/laʹd] 488

מִזְבֵּחַ altar [miz/bēʹaḥ] 401

מִי (interr.) who? [mî] 406

מָצָא find; (Hi) present [mā/ṣāʹ] 451

מִשְׁפָּט judgment, custom, justice [miš/pāʹṭ] 425

נָא (I) (part. of entreaty) pray, now; please [nāʾ] 401

נָפַל fall [nā/p̄aʹl] 433

עוֹד yet, still, again [ʻôd] 481

עוֹלָם, עֹלָם remote time; forever, eternity [ʻô/lāʹm; ʻō/lāʹm] 434

עַתָּה now [ʻat/tāʹ] 432

פֶּה; כְּפִי, לְפִי mouth; (conj.) according to [peh; kəp̄îʹ, ləp̄îʹ] 492

צָבָא (I) service in war; host, army [ṣā/bāʹ] 485

צִוָּה* (Pi) command [ṣā/wâʹ] 494

קֹדֶשׁ (adj., n.) holy (thing) [qōʹ/deš] 430

קוֹל voice, sound [qôl] 499

רַב (adj.) much, many (I?); (ctxt.) captain, chief (II?) [rab] 475

שַׂר official, leader, prince [śar] 412

שָׁאוּל Saul [šāʾ/ûʹl] 406

שֶׁבַע, שִׁבְעָה; (s. m., f.; pl.) seven; שִׁבְעִים (I) seventy [šeʹ/baʻ, šib/ʻâʹ; šib/ʻîʹm] 492

שָׁמַיִם heavens, sky [šā/maʹ/yim] 416

שָׁמַר keep watch, guard [šā/maʹr] 465

תָּוֶךְ; בְּתוֹךְ midst, middle; (prep.) within, through [tāʹ/wek; bətôk] 416

תַּחַת (I) (prep.) beneath, under, instead of [taʹ/ḥat] 490

32

B. Words Occurring 399 through 310 Times (29)

(I) אֹהֶל tent [ʼō'/hel] 342

אַהֲרוֹן Aaron [ʼa!/hărō'n] 347

אוֹ (conj.) or [ʼô] 311

(I) אֵשׁ fire [ʼēš] 375

אַתֶּם; אַתֶּן (pl. m.; f.) you [ʼat/tem; ʼat/ten] 330

בֵּין; בַּיִן (const. prep.) between; (n.) interval [bên; ba'/yin] 396

בָּנָה build [bā/ná'] 373

(II) בָּרַךְ bless [bā/rak] 328

דָּם blood [dām] 356

זָהָב gold [zā/há'b] 383

חַי; חַיִּים (n.) life (I), (adj.) living (II); (pl.) lifetime (I) [ḥai; ḥay/yi'm] 386

יָם sea; (ext.) west [yām] 392

יַעֲקֹב Jacob [ya!/ʻăqōb] 348

(I) יָרֵא (stat.) fear, be afraid [yā/rē'] 377

יָרַד go down [yā/ra'd] 380

כְּלִי vessel, utensil [kəli'] 324

כֶּסֶף silver [ke'/sep] 399

לֵוִי Levi (4x Aram.) [lē/wi'] 353

מִלְחָמָה war, battle [mil/ḥā/má'] 319

(I) מָלַךְ reign, be king [mā/la'k] 347

מָקוֹם place [mā/qô'm] 399

נְאֻם utterance, declaration [nə'u'm] 378

נָבִיא prophet [nā/bi'] 313

נָגַד* (Hi) make known, report, tell [nā/ḡa'd'] 369

(I) עָנָה answer [ʻā/ná'] 314

עֵץ (also coll.) tree [ʻēṣ] 330

רוּחַ spirit, wind [rú'aḥ] 376

שָׂדֶה; שָׂדַי open field [śā/de'h; śā/da'i] 332

(I) שַׁעַר gate [ša/ʻar] 368

C. Words Occurring 309 through 270 Times (26)

אֹיֵב, אוֹיֵב enemy [ʼō/yē'b; ʼô/yē'b] 281

(II) אַף nose, nostril; (ext.) anger [ʼap] 279

בָּבֶל; בַּבְלִי Babylon (Babel); (gent.) Babylonians [bā/be'l; bab/lā'i] 288

בְּרִית covenant [bəri't] 287

בָּשָׂר flesh [bā/śā'r] 270

(I) חֹדֶשׁ new moon, month [ḥō'/deš] 278

חָזַק be(come) strong; (Hi) seize, grasp [ḥā/za'q] 288

חַטָּאת sin, sin offering, expiation [ḥaṭ/ṭā't] 296

חָיָה live, be (stay) alive [ḥā/yâ'] 281

כָּרַת cut off, fell, exterminate; make (a covenant) [kā/ra't] 287

לֶחֶם bread [le'/ḥem] 296

מְאֹד (n.) force, might; (adv.) very, exceedingly [mə'ōd] 287

(I) מִדְבָּר pasturage, wilderness, steppe [mid/bā'r] 271

מִשְׁפָּחָה (extended) family; clan [miš/pā/ḥâ'] 300

סָבִיב (n.) circuit; (adv.) all around, round about, surrounding [sā/bî'b] 309

*סוּר turn aside; (Hi) take away, remove [sûrᵃ] 298

עָבַד work, serve, worship ['ā/ba'd] 289

(I) עֹלָה burnt offering ['ō/lā'] 288

עֵת time ['ēt] 282

פְּלִשְׁתִּי; פְּלֶשֶׁת (gent. n.) Philistine(s.); Philistia [pəliš/tî'; pəle'/šet] 294

פָּקַד visit, number, appoint; miss; take care of; muster [pā/qa'd] 301

פַּרְעֹה Pharaoh [par/'ō'h] 273

צֹאן; צֹנֶה flock [ṣō'n; ṣō/ne'h] 275

קָרַב draw near [qā/ra'b] 291

שְׁלֹמֹה Solomon [šəlō/mō'h] 293

(I) שֵׁשׁ, שִׁשָּׁה; שִׁשִּׁים (s. m., f.; pl.) six; sixty [šēš, šiš/šâ'; ši/ší'm] 272

D. Words Occuring 269 through 220 Times (31)

אֶבֶן (f.) stone ['e'/ben] 268

אַבְרָהָם; אַבְרָם Abraham; Abram ['ab/rā/hā'm; 'ab/rā'm] 235

(I) אֲדָמָה ground ['ădā/mā'] 225

(V) אֵל Mighty One, God (god) ['ēl] 236

(I) אַמָּה forearm, cubit ['am/mâ'] 226

*בָּקַשׁ (Pi) seek [bā/qa'šᵃ] 225

גְּבוּל boundary, territory [gəbúl] 241

זָכַר remember [zā/ka'r] 230

זֶרַע seed [ze'/ra'] 228

חָטָא miss (a mark), sin [ḥā/ṭā'] 237

חַיִל strength; wealth; army [ḥa'/yil] 246

(II) חֶסֶד loyalty, kindness, devotion, steadfast love [ḥe'/sed] 250

יְהוֹשׁוּעַ; יֵשׁוּעַ Joshua [yəhô/šú'a'; yē/šú'a'] 247

יָרַשׁ subdue, possess, dispossess (I?); tread (II?) [yā/ra'š] 231

יֹשֵׁב (Qal ptc.) inhabitant [yō/šē'b] 260

כָּתַב write [kā/ta'b] 222

לַיְלָה; לֵיל (m.) night [la'/yəlâ; la'/yil] 231

לְמַעַן (prep.) for the sake of, on account of; (conj.) in order that [ləma'/'an] 269

מוֹעֵד appointed place or time; season [mô/'ēd] 223

מַטֶּה rod, staff; (ext.) tribe [maṭ/ṭe'h] 252

מָלֵא (stat.) be full; (Pi) fill, fulfill [mā/lē'] 250

מַעֲשֶׂה work [ma/'ăśe'h] 235

(I) נַחֲלָה inheritance [na/ḥălâ'] 223

נַעַר lad, youth [na'/'ar] 240

עָוֹן transgression, iniquity ['ā/wō'n] 231

קֶרֶב; בְּקֶרֶב inward part, midst; (prep.) in (the midst of) [qe'/reb; bəqe'/reb] 227

(I) רָבָה be(come) numerous, be great; (Hi) multiply, make many [rā/bá'] 226

רֶגֶל foot [re'/ḡel] 252

רָשָׁע; רִשְׁעָה (s. m.; f.; adj.) guilty; (n.) wicked (one) [rā/šā''; rəšā/'â'] 264

שָׁלוֹם peace, health [šā/lô'm] 242

תּוֹרָה teaching, law [tô/rá'] 220

E. Words Occurring 219 through 200 Times (22)

אָהַב love, like ['ā/ha'b] 205

אֵם mother ['ēm] 219

אָסַף gather, take in ['ā/sa'p] 203

אָרוֹן ark, chest ['ărô'n] 202

(II) בֶּגֶד garment [be'/ḡed] 214

(II) בֹּקֶר morning [bō'/qer] 200

יוֹסֵף Joseph [yô/sē'p] 214

יָסַף add [yā/sa'p] 212

*יָשַׁע (Ni) be saved; (Hi) save [yā/ša''] 205

כָּבוֹד possessions, honor, glory [kā/bô'd] 200

*כּוּן (Ni) be firm, established; (Pol) establish; (Hi) prepare [kûn'] 219

(I) כָּלָה cease, come to an end, finish, complete [kā/lâ'] 204

מַחֲנֶה camp, army [ma/ḥăne'h] 219

מַלְאָךְ messenger [mal/ʾāʹk] 213

מִנְחָה gift; offering [min/ḥáʹ] 211

נָטָה turn, stretch out [nā/ṭáʹ] 215

נָצַל* (Ni) be delivered; (Hi) snatch away [nā/ṣalʹ] 208

(I) עָזַב leave, abandon [ʿā/zaʹb] 212

צַדִּיק (adj.) righteous, just [ṣad/dîʹq] 206

שָׁכַב lie down; have sexual intercourse [šā/kaʹb] 211

שָׁפַט judge, enter into controversy; (Ni) plead [šā/p̄aʹṭ] 203

(II) שָׁתָה (v.) drink [šā/ṭáʹ] 217

SECTION 3: HEBREW WORDS OCCURRING 199–100 TIMES (185)

A. Words Occurring 199 through 175 Times (24)

אָבַד perish; (Pi) destroy; (Hi) exterminate [ʾā/baḏ] 183

אֹזֶן ear [ʾṓ/zen] 187

אֶפְרַיִם; אֶפְרָתִי Ephraim; (gent.) Ephraimite [ʾep̄/ra/yim; ʾep̄/rā/tî́] 182

בְּהֵמָה; בְּהֵמוֹת cattle, animals; (pl. of ext.) crocodile? [bəhē/mấ; bəhē/môṯ] 192

בִּנְיָמִן; בֶּן־יְמִינִי Benjamin; (gent.) Benjamites [bin/yā/mín; ben-yəmî/nî́] 180

(I) בַּעַל owner, husband; Baʿal [baʿ/ʿal] 198

בָּקָר (coll.) cows, herd(s.), cattle [bā/qā́r] 183

גָּלָה reveal, uncover (I?); depart, go into captivity (II?) [gā/lấ] 187

זָקֵן (adj.) old; (n.) old man, elder [zā/qḗn] 178

חָצֵר permanent settlement, court, enclosure [ḥā/ṣḗr] 193

יָכֹל (stat.) be able [yā/kṓl] 194

יַרְדֵּן Jordan [yar/dḗn] 181

כַּף hand, palm [kap̄] 192

לָכֵן (adv.) therefore [lā/kḗn] 196

מוֹאָב; מוֹאָבִי Moab; (gent.) Moabite(s) [mô/ʾā́b; mô/ʾā/bî́] 199

מִצְוָה commandment [miṣ/wấ] 181

סֵפֶר scroll [sḗ/p̄er] 185

רִאשׁוֹן (ord.) first [ri ʾ/šṓn] 182

רוּם* be(come) high, exalted [rûm*] 195

(II) רֵעַ friend, fellow companion [rḗaʿ] 195

שָׂפָה lip; (ext.) shore [śā/p̄ấ] 178

שֵׁבֶט rod, staff; (ext.) tribe [šḗ/beṭ] 190

שָׁבַע* (Ni, Hi) swear [šā/baʿ*] 186

שֶׁמֶן oil [še/men] 193

B. Words Occurring 174 through 160 Times (27)

(I) אַחֵר (adj.) another [ʾa!/ḥḗr] 166

(I) אַיִל ram [ʾa/yil] 161

אַךְ (adv.) only; surely ['ak] 160

(I) בָּחַר choose [bā/ḥa'r] 173

בִּין* understand, perceive [bîn'] 171

גִּבּוֹר warrior, mighty man [gib/bô'r] 161

(II) דּוֹר generation, lifetime, life-span [dôr] 169

דָּרַשׁ seek [dā/ra'š] 163

הָרַג kill [hā/ra'g̱] 168

(I) זֶבַח (n.) sacrifice [ze'/baḥ] 162

(II) חָוָה* (Hisht) bow down [ḥā/wấ'] 174

חוּץ (n.) place outside the house, street; (prep., adv.) outside, without [ḥûṣ] 165

טָמֵא (stat.) be unclean [ṭā/mē''] 161

כְּנַעַן; כְּנַעֲנִי Canaan; (gent.) Canaanite [kəna'/'an; kəna!/'ănî'] 163

(I) לָחַם (Ni) fight [lā/ḥa'm] 171

לָמָּה, לָמֶה (interr. pron.) why? [lā'm/mâ, lā/mấ'] 173

מְלָאכָה work [məlā'/kấ'] 167

נוּס* flee [nûs''] 160

סָבַב turn around [sā/ba'b] 162

סָפַר write, count, number; (Pi) recount, report, enumerate [sā/p̄a'r] 162

עֶשֶׂר; עֲשָׂרָה (group of) ten, decade ['e'/śer; 'ā/śărấ'] 173

פֶּתַח gate, opening, entrance [pe'/taḥ] 163

קָדַשׁ be holy; (Pi) consecrate [qā/da'š] 172

(I) רָעָה feed, graze, tend (cattle) [rā/'ấ'] 171

שָׁאַל ask (for), demand [šā/'a'l] 173

שָׁחָה see (II) *174 חָוָה

שָׁחַת* (Ni) be corrupt, spoiled; (Pi) spoil, ruin; (Hi) destroy [šā/ḥa't''] 161

C. Words Occurring 159 through 144 Times (26)

אֲנַחְנוּ (pers. pron. c.) we ['ănaḥ/nú'] 156

אֲרָם ; אֲרַמִּי Aram, Syria; (gent.) Aramean(s), Syrian(s) ['ărā'm; 'ăram/mí'] 155

אַשּׁוּר Assyria (as gent.) Assyrian ['aš/šú'r] 152

(II) הָלַל* (Pi) praise; (Hith) boast [hā/la'l''] 145

חָכְמָה experience, shrewdness, wisdom [ḥok/mấ'] 152

יוֹאָב Joab [yô/'ā'b] 146

יִרְמְיָה; יִרְמְיָהוּ Jeremiah [yir/məyá'; yir/məyā'/hú] 147

כָּסָה* (Pi) cover, conceal [kā/sấ''] 157

לְבַד (adv.) alone; (prep.) besides [ləbad] 155

מָוֶת death [mắ/wet] 159

מְנַשֶּׁה Manasseh [mənaš/šéh] 150

נֶגֶד (n., prep., adv.) opposite, before (ne/ḡed] 151

נָגַע touch, reach; come to [nā/ḡaʿ] 150

נָסַע depart [nā/saʿ] 146

(I) עֵדָה congregation [ʿē/dắ] 149

פַּר; פָּרָה (m.; f.) young bull; cow [par; pā/rắ] 159

(I) פָּתַח open; (Pi) loosen, free [pā/taḥ] 144

צְדָקָה righteousness [ṣədā/qắ] 157

צִיּוֹן Zion [ṣiy/yốn] 154

(I) צָפוֹן north [ṣā/p̄ốn] 153

רֹב multitude, abundance [rōb] 153

שָׂמַח rejoice; (Pi) gladden [śā/maḥ] 156

שָׂנֵא hate; (Qal and Pi ptc.) adversary, enemy [śā/nēʾ] 148

(I) שָׁבַר break [šā/bar] 149

שְׁמֹנֶה, שְׁמֹנָה; שְׁמֹנִים (s. m., f.; pl.) eight; eighty [šəmō/néh, šəmō/nắ; šəmō/nî́m] 147

שֵׁנִי (ord.) second [šē/nî́] 156

D. Words Occurring 143 through 134 Times (26)

אָז; מֵאָז (adv.) then; formerly, since [ʾāz; mē/ʾắz] 141

זֶבַח slaughter, sacrifice; (Pi) sacrifice [zā/baḥ] 136

חָכָם (adj.) wise [ḥā/kắm] 138

(I) *חָלַל (Ni) be defiled; (Pi) pollute, profane; (Hi) begin [ḥā/laľ] 134

(I) חָנָה encamp [ḥā/nắ] 143

יַחַד; יַחְדָּו (n.) community; (adv.) together, at the same time [ya/ḥad; yaḥ/dắw] 142

יַיִן wine [ya/yin] 141

(I) יָמִין right hand/side; south [yā/mî́n] 139

יֵשׁ there is/are [yēš] 139

כְּמוֹ (rel. part.) just like [kəmốʾ] 139

כִּסֵּא seat, throne [kis/sḗʾ] 136

(I) מִסְפָּר (n.) number [mis/pắr] 134

(II) מַעַל (adj.) upwards; (prep.) above [ma/ʿal] 138

מִשְׁכָּן dwelling, tabernacle [miš/kān] 139

(I) נוּחַ (v.) rest, settle down, make quiet; (Hi) lay, deposit [nû́aḥ] 143

נַ֫חַל (I) torrent valley, wadi [naʹ/ḥal] 138

נְחֹ֫שֶׁת (I) copper, bronze [nəḥōʹ/šet] 139

סוּס; סוּסָה (I) (m.; f.) horse; mare [sûs; sûʹ/sấ] 139

עֲבוֹדָה service [ʽăbô/dấ] 143

עֶ֫רֶב (II) evening [ʽeʹ/reb] 134

פָּנָה turn about, turn aside [pā/nấ] 134

קָרָא (II) happen; (inf. const. as prep.) against [qā/rāʹ] 139

רָדַף pursue, persecute [rā/dāp̄] 143

שֶׁ־ (pref. rel. part.) who, which; that (with dagesh in following cons.) 139

שְׁמוּאֵל Samuel [šəmû/ʼēʹl] 139

שֶׁ֫מֶשׁ sun [šeʹ/meš] 134

E. Words Occurring 133 through 121 Times (28)

אוֹר light [ʼôr] 125

אֱמֶת trustworthiness, stability, truth [ʼĕmet] 127

אַף (I) (conj.) also, even, the more so [ʼap̄] 130

בּוֹשׁ (I) be ashamed [bôš] 126

בְּכֹר, בְּכוֹר firstborn [bəkōr, bəkôr] 122

גָּדַל be(come) strong, great; (Pi) bring up, let grow, nourish [gā/daʹl] 122

חוֹמָה (city) wall [ḥô/mấ] 133

חִזְקִיָּה; חִזְקִיָּ֫הוּ Hezekiah [ḥiz/qiy/yấ; ḥiz/qiy/yāʹ/hû] 131

חֵמָה heat; rage, wrath; poison [ḥē/mấ] 126

חֲצִי half [ḥăṣiʹ] 123

חֹק prescription, rule [ḥōq] 128

חָשַׁב (v.) account, regard, value [ḥā/šaʹb] 124

יְהוֹנָתָן Jonathan [yəhô/nā/tấn] 124

כֶּ֫בֶשׂ; כִּבְשָׂה (m.; f.) young ram; ewe-lamb [keʹ/beś; kib/śấ] 129

כֹּחַ (I) strength, power [kōʹaḥ] 125

כִּשְׂבָּה; כֶּ֫שֶׂב Cf. כֶּ֫בֶשׂ [keʹ/śeb; kiś/bấ] 129

לָכַד seize, capture [lā/kaʹd] 121

נָגַשׁ draw near, approach [nā/ḡaš] 125

נָשִׂיא (I) prince [nā/śîʹ] 133

עַמּוֹן; עַמּוֹנִי Ammon; (gent.) Ammonites [ʽam/môʹn; ʽam/mô/nîʹ] 122

עֶ֫צֶם (I) (s., coll.) bone [ʽeʹ/ṣem] 123

פֶּן־ (conj.) lest [pen-] 133

קָבַץ assemble, gather together [qā/baṣ] 127

קָבַר bury [qā/bar] 132

קָהָל assembly, congregation [qā/hā'l] 123

שָׁאַר remain; (Ni, Hi) be left over [šā/'ar] 133

שָׁכַן (v.) tent, dwell, settle [šā/ka'n] 130

שָׁלַךְ* (Hi) throw, cast [šā/la'k] 125

F. Words Occurring 120 through 112 Times (27)

אֱדוֹם; אֲדוֹמִי Edom; (gent.) Edomite(s) ['ĕdô'm; 'ădô/mî'] 112

אָחוֹת sister ['ā/ḥô't] 114

בָּטַח (I) trust; fall to the ground? be reckless (II?) [bā/ṭaḥ] 119

בָּכָה weep [bā/ká'] 114

יָדָה* (II) (Pi) throw, cast; (Hi, Hith) thank, praise, confess [yā/dá'] 115

יָטַב be good (cf. טוֹב, 4.B; (I) טוֹב, 1.D) [yā/ṭa'b] 120

יִצְחָק Isaac [yiṣ/ḥā'q] 112

יָשָׁר (adj.) straight, right, upright [yā/šā'r] 119

כָּבֵד (stat.) be heavy, honored [kā/bē'd] 114

לָבַשׁ put on, clothe [lā/ba'š] 113

לִקְרַאת (inf. const. as prep.) over against, opposite [liq/ra't] 120

לָשׁוֹן tongue [lā/šô'n] 117

מִגְרָשׁ pasture, untilled ground; produce [miḡ/rā'š] 115

מַמְלָכָה kingdom [mam/lā/ká'] 117

נָבָא* (Ni, Hith) prophesy [nā/bā'] 115

נָהָר river, stream [nā/hā'r] 117

פְּרִי fruit; offspring [pərî] 119

צֶדֶק righteousness; what is right, just [ṣe'/deq] 116

קָדוֹשׁ (adj.) holy [qā/dô'š] 115

קָטַר* (Pi) send an offering up in smoke; (Hi) make smoke [qā/ṭa'r] 116

רֶכֶב chariot, chariotry [re'/keb] 120

שָׂרַף burn [śā/ra'p] 117

שָׁלֵם (stat.) be whole, complete; (Pi) repay; (Hi) make peace with [šā/lē'm] 117

שֹׁמְרוֹן Samaria (2x Aram.) [šōm/rô'n] 112

שָׁפַךְ pour out [šā/pa'k] 116

שֶׁקֶר lie, falsehood, deception [šeʹ/qer] 113

תּוֹעֵבָה abomination [tô/ʿē/bāʹ] 118

G. Words Occurring 111 through 100 Times (27)

אַבְשָׁלוֹם Absalom [ʾab/šā/lôʹm] 107

(I)* אָמֵן (Ni) be steady, firm, trustworthy, faithful; (Hi) believe [ʾā/mēʹnʿ] 100

בִּלְתִּי (n.) non-existence; (adv.) not; (prep.) except [bil/tîʹ] 111

בָּמָה high place, funerary installation [bā/māʹ] 103

(I) בַּעַד; בְּעַד (n.) distance; (prep.) behind, through, for (the benefit of) [baʹ/ʿad; bə/ʿad] 101

(I) גָּאַל redeem [gā/ʾalʹ] 104

גִּלְעָד; גִּלְעָדִי Gilead; (gent.) Gildeadites [gil/ʿāʹd; gil/ʿā/dîʹ] 108

(I) הֵן (dem. interj.) behold!; (conj.) if (cf. הִנֵּה, 1.B) [hēn] 100

חֻקָּה statute, prescription [ḥuq/qāʹ] 104

יָרָבְעָם Jeroboam [yā/rob/ʿāʹm] 104

יָתַר* (Ni, Hi) be left, remain [yā/taʹr] 106

כָּנָף wing [kā/nāʹp] 110

כָּפַר cover; (Pi ext.) expiate [kā/paʹr] 102

מַרְאֶה sight, appearance [mar/ʾeʹh] 103

נֶגֶב the dry country; south, Negev [neʹ/ḡeb] 110

נָחַם* (Ni) be sorry, repent; (Pi) comfort, console [nā/ḥaʹmʿ] 108

עַמּוּד pillar, column [ʿam/mûʹd] 111

עָפָר dry earth, dust [ʿā/pāʹr] 110

פַּעַם foot, step; time [paʹ/ʿam] 111

רוּץ* run [rûṣ] 103

רֹחַב breadth [rō/ḥab] 101

רָעָב hunger, famine [rā/ʿāʹb] 103

(II) רַק (adv.) only [raq] 108

שַׁבָּת sabbath, rest [šab/bāʹt] 106

שָׁכַח forget [šā/kaʹḥ] 102

שְׁלִישִׁי (ord.) third; (fract.) one-third [šəli/šîʹ] 107

תָּמִיד (n.) continuance; (adv.) continually, regularly [tā/mîʹd] 104

SECTION 4: HEBREW WORDS OCCURRING 99–50 TIMES (313)

A. Words Occurring 99 through 93 Times (26)

אַחְאָב Ahab [ʾaḥ/ʾāʹb] 93

אֹרֶךְ length [ʾōʹ/rek] 95

גֵּר stranger [gēr] 93

הָפַךְ turn, overturn [hā/p̄aʹk] 95

זָנָה commit fornication; play the harlot [zā/nāʹ] 95

(I) חַיָּה (s. or pl. coll.) animals [ḥay/yāʹ] 97

חָלָל (n., adj.) slain, struck dead [ḥā/lāʹl] 94

(I) חֲמוֹר (male) ass [ḥămôʹr] 97

(I) חָרָה be(come) hot, burning, angry [ḥā/rāʹ] 94

טָהוֹר (adj.) clean, pure [ṭā/hôʹr] 94

טָהֵר be clean, pure [ṭā/hēʹr] 94

יַעַן (prep.) on account of; (conj.) because [yaʹ/ʿan] 93

(I) יֶתֶר remainder [yeʹ/ter] 96

(I) כֶּרֶם vineyard [keʹ/rem] 93

(I) מָלַט* (Ni) escape; (Pi) save, deliver [mā/laṭʹ] 95

מְעַט (adj.) (a) few; (n.) a little [mə/ʿaṭ] 96

עוֹר skin, leather [ʿôr] 99

עֹז, עַז strength, power, might [ʿōz, ʿāz] 94

עֵשָׂו Esau [ʿē/śāʹw] 96

פֶּשַׁע rebellion, revolt, transgression [peʹ/šaʿ] 93

(I) רָעַע be wicked, evil [rā/ʿaʿ] 99

שָׂבַע satisfy, be satiated [śā/baʿ] 97

שִׂמְחָה joy, rejoicing [śim/ḥāʹ] 94

שְׁבִיעִי (ord.) seventh [šəbî/ʿîʹ] 96

שָׁמֵם (stat.) be astonished; be desolate [šā/mēʹm] 95

שָׁרַת* (Pi) minister to, serve [šā/raʹt] 98

B. Words Occurring 92 through 86 Times (31)

אֱמֹרִי (gent.) Amorite(s) [ʾĕmō/rîʹ] 86

בָּעַר consume, burn (I?); graze (II?) [bā/ʿaʹr] 87

דֶּלֶת door [deʹ/let] 87

דַּעַת knowledge [da'/'at] 91

הָמוֹן tumult, turmoil, multitude [hā/mốn] 86

זְרוֹעַ arm, forearm [zərố'a'] 91

(I) חֵלֶב fat [ḥē'/leb] 92

(I) חָפֵץ please, delight, take pleasure [ḥā/pē'ṣ] 86

*טוֹב be good, pleasant (cf. יָטַב 3.F; (I) טוֹב, 1.D) [ṭôb"] 90

טָמֵא; טְמֵאָה (adj., m.; f.) unclean [ṭā/mē'; ṭəmē/'â'] 88

יְהוֹשָׁפָט Jehoshaphat [yəhô/šā/pā'ṭ] 86

יֶלֶד; יַלְדָּה (s. m.; f.) male child, boy; girl [ye'/led; yal/dā'] 92

(I) כְּרוּב cherub [kərûb] 92

(I) כַּשְׂדִּים Chaldea; (gent.) Chaldean (9x Aram.) [kaś/dî'm] 89

מַלְכוּת dominion; kingdom [mal/kû't] 91

נְבוּכַדְנֶאצַּר Nebuchadnezzar (spelled 5 ways in MT; 31x Aram.) [nəbû/kad/ne'ṣ/ṣa'r] 91

סָגַר shut, close; (Hi) deliver up, give in one's power [sā/ḡa'r] 90

(I) עֵבֶר side, region; opposite side ['ē'/ber] 91

(I) עָנָן clouds ['ā/nā'n] 86

(I) עֵצָה advice, counsel ['ē/ṣâ'] 89

פֵּאָה side, rim, corner; piece? (II?); luxury? (III?) [pē/'â'] 86

קֶדֶם; קֵדְמָ in front, east; east(ward) [qe'/dem; qē'/dem] 87

קָצֶה end, border, extremity [qā/ṣe'h] 90

רְאוּבֵן; רְאוּבֵנִי Reuben; (gent.) Reubenite [rə'û/bē'n; rə'û/bē/nî'] 87

*שִׁיר sing [šîr"] 88

שִׁיר; שִׁירָה (m.; f.) song [šîr; šî/rā'] 91

*שִׁית put, place [šît"] 87

שֶׁלֶם final (or peace) offering [še'/lem] 87

*שָׁמַד (Ni) be destroyed, exterminated; (Hi) exterminate [šā/ma'd"] 90

שֶׁקֶל shekel (unit of weight) [še'/qel] 88

תָּמִים (adj.) whole, entire; blameless [tā/mî'm] 91

C. Words Occurring 85 through 79 Times (27)

אָוֶן wickedness, iniquity ['ā'/wen] 80

אוֹצָר supply, store-house, treasure ['ô/ṣā'r] 79

אוֹת (I) sign [ʾôt] 79

אֲרִי; אַרְיֵה (m.; m. and f.) lion [ʾărî; ʾar/ʾēh] 83

גָּד; גָּדִי Gad; (gent.) Gadites [gād; gā/dî] 85

גּוּר* (I) sojourn [gûr] 81

דָּנִיֵּאל Daniel (52x Aram. section of Daniel) [dā/niy/yē'l] 81

הֵיכָל palace, temple [hê/kā'l] 80

זָכָר man; male (animal) [zā/kā'r] 82

חֹשֶׁךְ darkness [ḥō'/šek] 82

יָעַץ give counsel, advice [yā/ʿaṣ] 82

לָמַד learn; (Pi) teach [lā/ma'd] 85

מָהַר* (I) (Pi) hasten [mā/har] 83

מָכַר sell [mā/ka'r] 81

מָשַׁל (II) rule, govern [mā/šal] 82

סָתַר* (Ni, intrans.) conceal, hide; (Hi, trans.) hide (someone) [sā/ta'r] 83

עֵדוּת; עֵדָה (III) warning sign, reminder; precept, commandment [ʿē/dú't; ʿē/dâ'] 83

עָזַר help, assist [ʿā/za'r] 82

עָנָה (II) bend down, be afflicted, humble; (Pi) oppress, humiliate [ʿā/nâ'] 79

פָּלַל* (II) (Hith) pray [pā/la'l] 80

קָלַל be slight, trifling, swift; (Pi) declare cursed; (Hi) make light [qā/la'l] 82

קָרְבָּן offering, gift [qor/bā'n] 80

רָחוֹק (adj.) far, distant; (n.) distance [rā/ḥô'q] 85

רֹעֶה (Qal ptc.) shepherd [rō/ʿe'h] 84

שׁוֹר bull(ock), steer [šôr] 79

שָׁחַט (I) slaughter, kill [šā/ḥa'ṭ] 85

שָׁקָה* (Hi) give to drink [šā/qâ'] 79

D. Words Occurring 78 through 75 Times (28)

בַּרְזֶל iron [bar/ze'l] 76

גּוֹרָל lot; (ext.) allotment [gô/rā'l] 78

דָּן; דָּנִי Dan; (gent.) Danites [dān; dānî'] 78

חֶבְרוֹן Hebron [ḥeb/rô'n] 77

חָלָה be(come) weak, sick [ḥā/lâ'] 77

חָנַן (I) be gracious to, favor; (Hith) implore favor or compassion [ḥā/na'n] 77

יְשׁוּעָה deliverance, salvation [yəšû/ʿâ'] 78

מָאַס (I) reject [mā/ʾás] 75

מָאתַיִם (d.) two hundred [mā'/ta'/yim] 77

מִקְנֶה possession (of land, cattle) [miq/neʹh] 76

מִשְׁמֶרֶת (n.) guard, obligation, service [miš/me'/ret] 78

נֶגַע blow, assault; plague [ne'/ḡaʻ] 78

נָצַב* (Ni) take one's stand, be stationed (I?); wretched? (II?) [nā/ṣa'b] 75

עוּר* (III) arouse, awake [ʻûr'] 76

עָנִי (adj.) afflicted, poor [ʻā/ni'] 76

עָרַךְ arrange, set in order [ʻā/ra'k] 75

צוּר (I) boulder, (large) rock [ṣûr] 75

צָר (II) adversary, foe [ṣar] 76

קָנָה (I) acquire, buy [qā/nâ'] 78

קָרוֹב; קְרוֹבָה (adj. m.; f.) near, imminent [qā/rô'b; qərô/bá'] 78

קֶרֶן horn [qe'/ren] 76

קֶשֶׁת bow (weapon); (met.) rainbow [qe'/šet] 76

רָכַב ride [rā/ka'b] 78

שָׂכַל (I) have success; (Hi) understand [śā/ka'l] 75

שָׁלָל plunder, booty [šā/lā'l] 76

תְּפִלָּה prayer [təp̄il/lá'] 78

תְּרוּמָה tribute, contribution, heave-offering [tərû/mâ'] 77

תֵּשַׁע, תִּשְׁעָה; תִּשְׁעִים (s., m., f.; pl.) nine; ninety [tē'/šaʻ, tiš/'â'; tiš/'î'm] 77

E. Words Occurring 74 through 71 Times (28)

אֵלִיָּה, אֵלִיָּהוּ Elijah [ʾē/liy/yâ', ʾē/liy/yā'/hú] 71

אֶלְעָזָר Eleazar [ʾel/ʻā/zā'r] 72

אָסַר bind; (Ni, Pu) be fettered, imprisoned [ʾā/sa'r] 71

אֶרֶז (trad.) cedar [ʾe'/rez] 73

בֶּטֶן belly, womb [be'/ṭen] 72

בְּרָכָה (I) blessing [bərā/kâ'] 71

גָּבַה (stat.) be high [gā/ba'h] 74

הֶבֶל (I) breath; vanity, idol(s) [he'/bel] 73

זָעַק cry out; (Ni) called to arms (cf. צָעַק, 4.J) [zā/'a'q] 73

זָר (adj.) strange, different; illicit [zār] 71

חָזָה see, perceive [ḥā/zá'] 72

חֶרְפָּה reproach, disgrace [ḥer/pâ'] 73

לְבָנוֹן Lebanon [ləbā/nô'n] 71

לִין* spend the night, lodge [lîn"] 71

מַדּוּעַ (interr. adv.) wherefore? why? [mad/dú'aʿ] 72

מִזְרָח sunrise, east [mis/rā'ḥ] 74

מִקְדָּשׁ sanctuary [miq/dā'š] 74

מֵת (adj.) dead [mēt] 72

סֶלָה selah (unexplained technical term of music or recitation) [se'/lâ] 74

(II) עֵד; עֵדָה (m.; f.) witness [ʿēd; ʿē/dâ'] 72

עוֹף (coll.) flying creatures; fowl, insects [ʿôp] 71

עֵז goat, goathair [ʿēz] 74

(I) פָּלָא* (Ni) be extraordinary, wonderful [pā/lā''"] 71

(I) צָרָה distress [ṣā/rā'] 72

(I) קִיר wall [qîr] 74

רָחַץ wash (oneself) [rā/ḥaṣ] 72

שָׁבַת cease, rest [šā/ba't] 71

שׁוֹפָר ram's horn, trumpet [šô/pā'r] 72

F. Words Occurring 70 through 66 Times (28)

אֲבִימֶלֶךְ Abimelech [ʾăbî/me'/lek] 67

אֲחֻזָּה landed property [ʾăḥuz/zā'] 66

אַלּוּף (adj.) familiar; (n.) confidant (I); tribal chief (II) [ʾal/lú'p] 69

בּוֹר cistern [bôr] 69

בֵּית(־)אֵל Bethel [bêt(-)'ē'l] 70

בַּל (neg.) not; surely? (II?) [bal] 66

(I) גֶּבֶר young man; strong man [ge'/ber] 66

חֲלוֹם dream [ḥălôm] 66

חֵן charm, favor; grace [ḥēn] 68

כִּכָּר loaf of bread; talent; environs (all circular) [kik/kā'r] 67

(I) כְּסִיל (adj.) insolent (spiritual); stupid, dull (practical things) [kəsîl] 70

כְּפִי; לְפִי (conj.) according to, as; so that [kəpî'; ləpî'] 67

כָּתֵף shoulder(-blade) [kā/tē'p] 67

לְפִי Cf. כְּפִי

מִדְיָן; מִדְיָנִי Midian; (gent.) Midianite (II) [mid/yā'n; mid/yā/nî'] 67

מָלֵא (adj., n., pred. adj.) full [mā/lē''] 67

מָשַׁח anoint [mā/šáḥ] 70

נָבַט* (Pi, Hi) look at, regard [nā/baṭ] 70

עֵמֶק valley ['ē/meq] 68

פֹּה; פּוֹ; פֹּא here [pōh; pô; pō'] 68

פָּרַשׂ (trans.) spread out; (met.) flaunt [pā/ráś] 67

קֶבֶר grave [qe/ber] 67

קָדִים east side, east [qā/dím] 69

קֵץ end; limit, boundary [qēṣ] 67

רָפָא heal (someone) [rā/pā'] 67

שְׁאֵרִית remainder [šə'ē/rít] 66

שֻׁלְחָן table [šul/ḥā'n] 70

תָּקַע drive, thrust; strike [tā/qá'] 67

G. Words Occurring 65 through 63 Times (24)

אַבְנֵר Abner ['ab/nē'r] 63

אָחַז (I) seize, hold fast ['ā/ḥá'z] 63

אִשֶּׁה offering by fire ['iš/šé'h] 65

בִּלְעָם (I) Balaam [bil/'ā'm] 64

גִּבְעָה (I) hill; (cultic) high place [gib/'á'] 65

חֵלֶק (II) part, portion [ḥē'/leq] 65

יְאֹר (great) river (Nile, Euphrates) [yə'ōr] 64

יוֹאָשׁ Joash [yô/'ā'š] 64

יָצַר form, shape, fashion [yā/ṣár] 64

כָּשַׁל stumble, totter [kā/šál] 63

מִיכָה, מִיכָא; מִיכָיְהוּ Micah [mî/kấ, mî/kā'; mî/kā/yəhû'] 63

נַעֲרָה (I) young girl, maid [na!/'ărấ] 63

נָצַח* (Pi) lead; supervise [nā/ṣaḥ] 65

נָצַר watch, guard [nā/ṣár] 63

פּוּץ* (intrans.) scatter, disperse [pûṣ] 65

צִדְקִיָּה; צִדְקִיָּהוּ Zedekiah [ṣid/qiy/yấ; ṣid/qiy/yā'/hû] 63

צָלַח (be) strong, effective; succeed [ṣā/lá'ḥ] 65

רִיב* contend, plead (a case) [rîb] 64

שְׁאוֹל sheol, underworld [šə'ôl] 65

שָׁכַם* (den.; Hi) rise early [šā/ká'm] 65

שְׁכֶם (II) Shechem [šəkem] 64

שִׁפְחָה female slave [šip/ḥá'] 63

תָּמַם be complete [tā/má'm] 64

תָּפַשׂ seize, take hold of [tā/pá'š] 64

H. Words Occurring 62 through 58 times (31)

אֶבְיוֹן (adj.) poor, oppressed [ʾeb/yôʹn] 61

אַחֲרִית end, outcome [ʾa!/ḥărîʹt] 61

אִיּוֹב Job [ʾiy/yôʹb] 58

אֵיךְ (interr.) how? (cf אֵיכָה, 5.V) [ʾêk] 60

אֱלִישָׁע Elisha [ʾĕlî/šāʹʿ] 58

אָסָא Asa [ʾā/sāʹ] 58

אֵצֶל (n.) side; (prep.) beside [ʾēʹ/ṣel] 61

אָרַר curse [ʾā/raʹr] 59

בָּרַח (I) run away, flee [bā/raʹḥ] 62

בָּשָׁן Bashan [bā/šāʹn] 60

גְּבוּרָה strength [gəbû/rāʹ] 62

דּוֹד beloved, lover [dôd] 59

דָּרַךְ tread; (Hi) stamp firm [dā/raʹk] 61

חַג; חָג procession; feast, festival [ḥāḡ; ḥaḡ] 60

חָמָס violence, wrong [ḥā/māʹs] 60

חֵת; חִתִּי Heth; (gent.) Hittite(s) [ḥēt; ḥit/tîʹ] 62

יֵהוּא Jehu [yē/hûʹ] 58

מָגֵן (I) shield [mā/ḡēʹn] 59

מָרְדְּכַי Mordecai [mor/dŏkaʹi] 60

נֶדֶר, נֵדֶר vow [neʹ/der, nēʹ/der] 60

נָחַל obtain, receive property [nā/ḥaʹl] 59

נֶסֶךְ, נֵסֶךְ (I) libation [neʹ/sek, nēʹ/sek] 60

עֲרָבָה (II) desert, plain [ʿărā/bāʹ] 61

צָרַר wrap up (I); be hostile toward (II) (cf (I), צוּר 5.J) [ṣā/raʹr] 61

קְטֹרֶת smoke (of sacrifice); incense [qəṭōʹ/ret] 61

קָנֶה (measuring) reed, tube [qā/neʹh] 62

קָרַע tear up, away [qā/raʹʿ] 62

רִיב*; רִיבָה (m.; f. pl.) contention, suit; legal speech [rîb; rî/bāʹ] 62

רֵיחַ odor, scent [rêʹaḥ] 59

שֹׁפֵט (n., Qal ptc. act.) judge [šō/pēʹṭ] 58

תְּהִלָּה glory, praise [təhil/lāʹ] 58

I. Words Occurring 57 through 55 Times (34)

אֶדֶן* (pl.) pedestal, socket [ʾeʹ/den*] 55

אַלְמָנָה widow [ʾal/mā/nāʹ] 55

אָמָה female slave [ʾā/māʹ] 56

אֶסְתֵּר Esther [ʾes/tēʹr] 55

אֹרַח way, path [ʾōʹ/raḥ] 57

גֶּפֶן vine [ge'/p̄en] 55

זֶרַע sow [zā/raʿ] 56

חָזָק (adj.) hard, strong [ḥā/zā'q] 56

(I) חִיל* be in labor [ḥil'] 57

(II) חָלַק divide, apportion; (Pi) scatter (III?) [ḥā/la'q] 56

טֶרֶם; בְּטֶרֶם (neg.) not yet; (conj., prep.) before [ṭe'/rem; bəṭe'/rem] 56

יָבֵשׁ (stat.) be dry; (intrans.) dry up [yā/bē'š] 55

יְהוֹיָדָע Jehoiada [yəhô/yā/dā'ʿ] 56

יָכַח* (Ni) dispute; (Hi) reprove [yā/kaḥ'] 56

(I) יַעַר thicket [ya'/ʿar] 57

יְרִחוֹ Jericho [yəri/ḥô'] 57

יִשְׁמָעֵאל; Ishmael; (gent.)
יִשְׁמְעֵאלִי Ishmaelite [yiš/mā/'ē'l; yiš/mə'ē'/lî'] 56

מִזְמוֹר psalm [miz/mô'r] 57

מַחֲשָׁבָה thought [ma!/ḥăšā/bâ'] 56

מְנַצֵּחַ conductor? (Pi ptc. of נָצַח) [mənaṣ/ṣē'aḥ] 57

נָטַע (v.) plant [nā/ṭaʿ'] 57

סֶלַע rock [se'/laʿ] 57

סֹפֵר scribe, writer [sō/p̄ē'r] 55

(I) עָמָל distress, trouble; effort [ʿā/mā'l] 55

פָּדָה buy (off), ransom [pā/dâ'] 56

פָּעַל make, do [pā/ʿa'l] 57

פָּרָשׁ horsemen; horse (pā/rā'š] 57

רְבִיעִי (ord.) fourth; (fract.) one-fourth [rəbî/ʿî'] 55

רָחַק be(come) far (away), distant [rā/ḥa'q] 57

(II) רָמָה Ramah [rā/mâ'] 57

רָצוֹן pleasure; favor [rā/ṣô'n] 56

שָׂעִיר (n.) he-goat (III); (adj.) hairy (I) [śā/ʿî'r] 55

שָׁדַד devastate, lay waste [šā/da'd] 56

שְׁמָמָה horror, desolation [šəmā/mâ'] 56

J. Words Occurring 54 and 53 Times (29)

אָבָה accede, accept [ʾā/bâ'] 54

אֱמוּנָה steadiness [ʾĕmû/nâ'] 53

גָּמָל camel [gā/mā'l] 54

דָּבַק stick, cling to [dā/ba'q] 54

דְּבַשׁ honey [dəbaš] 54

הָמָן Haman [hā/mā'n] 54

(I) חָדַל cease, desist [ḥā/da'l] 53

חָדָשׁ (adj.) new, fresh [ḥā/dā'š] 53

חֵץ arrow [ḥēṣ] 54

חָתַת be shattered; (ext.) filled with terror [ḥā/ta' t] 53

יָצַק dish up (food); pour out (liquid) [yā/ṣa'q] 53

יָרָה* (III) (Hi) instruct, teach [yā/râ''] 54

יְרִיעָה curtain, tent (fabric) [yərî/'â'] 54

כּוּשׁ; כּוּשִׁי Cush; (gent.) Cushite [kûš; kû/šî'] 54

כָּעַס (be) irritated, angry [kā/'as] 54

לָבָן (II) Laban [lā/bā'n] 54

מִדָּה (I) (n.) measure [mid/dâ'] 53

מַצָּה (I) unleavened bread [maṣ/ṣâ'] 53

מָרוֹם height [mā/rô'm] 54

סֹלֶת fine wheat flour [sō'/let] 53

עֶלְיוֹן upper; Most High ['el/yô'n] 53

עֶרְוָה nakedness ['er/wâ'] 53

צָדוֹק Zadok [ṣā/dô'q] 53

צֵל shadow, shade [ṣēl] 53

צָעַק cry out (cf. זָעַק, 4.E) [ṣā/'a'q] 54

קָטֹן (adj.) small, insignificant [qā/ṭō'n] 54

שְׂמֹאל left (side); left hand [śəmō'l] 54

שָׂרָה; שָׂרַי (II) Sarah; Sarai [śā/râ'; śā/ra'i] 53

שֵׁן tooth; (ext.) crag [šēn] 53

K. Words Occurring 52 through 50 Times (27)

אַחֲרוֹן (adj.) behind; (adv.) last ['a!/ḥărô'n] 50

אַיֵּה (interr.) where? ['ay/yē'h] 52

אֵילָם; אוּלָם vestibule ['ê/lā'm; 'û/lā'm] 50

בָּקַע (v.) split [bā/qa'] 51

בְּתוּלָה virgin [bətû/lâ'] 51

חָרַם (I) devote to the ban [ḥā/ra'm] 51

יֹאשִׁיָּה, יֹאשִׁיָּהוּ Josiah [yō/šiy/yâ', yō'/šiy/yā'/hú] 51

יוֹמָם in the daytime [yô/mā'm] 51

כָּבַס full (cloth); (Pi) wash [kā/ba's] 51

מָדַד (v.) measure [mā/da'd] 52

מוּסָר chastening, correction [mû/sā'r] 50

מָחָר tomorrow [mā/ḥā'r] 52

נָדַח* (I) (Ni) be scattered [nā/da'ḥ] 51

נָכַר* (Ni) pretend; (Hi) investigate, recognize [nā/ka'r] 50

נַפְתָּלִי Naphtali [nap/tā/lî'] 50

נָשַׂג* (Hi) overtake [nā/śáḡʷ] 50

עֲמָלֵק; עֲמָלֵקִי Amalek; (gent.) Amalekite ['ămā/lḗq; 'ămā/lē/qî'] 51

פָּרַץ make a breach; burst out [pā/ráṣ] 50

פָּרַר* (Hi) break out, burst forth; shake (II?) [pā/rár̄] 50

קֶרֶשׁ plank [qé/reš] 51

רֵאשִׁית beginning, first [rē'/šî't] 51

רְחַבְעָם Rehoboam [rəhab/'ā'm] 50

רָנַן shout (for joy) [rā/nán] 52

רָצָה (I) be pleased with; like [rā/ṣá'] 50

שָׁוְא (adj., n.) worthless(ness); (adv.) in vain [šāw'] 52

תָּעָה wander off, stagger [tā/'á'] 50

תִּפְאֶרֶת (f.) ornament, decoration [tiṗ/'é/ret] 51

SECTION 5: HEBREW WORDS OCCURRING 49–10 TIMES (1248)

A. Words Occurring 49 and 48 Times (30)

(I) אֹמֶר saying, word ['ē'/mer] 49

(I) אֵפֹד ephod (priestly garment; cult object) ['ē/p̄ō'd] 49

בָּגַד treat faithlessly [bā/ḡá'd] 49

בַּעֲבוּר on account of, for the sake of, because of, in order that [ba!/ʿăbú'r] 49

(I) בָּרָא create [bā/rā'] 48

גָּאוֹן loftiness; pride [gā/'ô'n] 49

גִּלּוּל (pl.) idols [gil/lû'l] 48

(I) דֶּבֶר (bubonic) plague [de'/ber] 49

(II) דַּל (adj.) mean, scanty; (n.) poor [dal] 48

הוֹי (interj.) alas! woe! [hôy] 48

(I) הֵנָּה (adv.; spacial) hither, here; (temp.) until now [hē'n/nâ] 49

הַרְבֵּה (adv.) great number, many, much [har/bē'h] 49

(II) חֶבֶל rope; (ext.) measure, plot [ḥe'/bel] 49

טַבַּעַת ring, signet-ring [ṭab/ba'/ʿat] 49

יָצַב (Hith) take one's stand, position, stand (firm); appear, arrive [yā/ṣab] 48

(I) מִגְדָּל tower [miḡ/dā'l] 49

מַכָּה blow, wound [mak/kâ'] 48

מִשְׁקָל weight [miš/qā'l] 49

נְבֵלָה corpse [nəbē/lâ'] 48

נָגַף injure, strike [nā/ḡa'p̄] 49

סָמַךְ support [sā/ma'k] 48

(I) *עֲבוּר (alw. with pref. בַּ־) Cf. בַעֲבוּר ['ăbûr*] 49

(I) עַד eternity, always ['ad] 48

(I) פַּחַד trembling, terror [pa'/ḥad] 49

פֶּסַח Passover (festival, sacrifice) [pe'/saḥ] 49

(I) קָצִיר crop, harvest [qā/ṣî'r] 49

שַׂק goathair cloth, sackcloth; sack [śaq] 48

שְׁבִי (those who are/that which is) taken captive [šəbî] 48

שַׁדַּי (adj.) Almighty [šad/dá'i] 48

תְּכֵלֶת purple wool [təkē'/let] 49

B. Words Occurring 47 and 46 Times (26)

אָשָׁם guilt, wrong; guilt offering ['ā/šā'm] 46

גֹּאֵל redeemer [gō/'ē'l] 46

גַּיְא valley [gay'] 47

גָּרַשׁ banish, divorce, drive out (I?); toss up (II?) [gā/ra'š] 47

חֲנִית spear [ḥănî't] 47

(II) חָרֵשׁ (stat.) be deaf; (Hi) be silent [ḥā/rē'š] 47

לִשְׁכָּה hall [liš/kå'] 47

מָאֵן* (Pi) refuse, refuse to [mā/'a'n*] 46

מַעֲלָה ascent [ma!/'ălå'] 47

מִשְׁכָּב couch, bed [miš/kā'b] 46

מִשְׁתֶּה (drinking-) feast [miš/te'h] 46

מָתְנַיִם (d.) loins [mot/na'/yim] 47

נָכְרִי (adj.) foreign, strange; (n.) foreigner [nok/rî'] 46

נְעוּרִים youth [nə'û/rî'm] 47

סָלַח forgive [sā/la'ḥ] 46

(I) עֵזֶר; עֶזְרָה (s. m.; f.) support, help, (ext. or coll.) helper(s) ['ē'/zer; 'ez/rå'] 47

עָצַר restrain, detain ['ā/ṣa'r] 46

פָּגַע encounter, meet; entreat [pā/ḡa'] 46

(II) צָפָה arrange; (Pi) overlay [ṣā/p̄ā'] 46

(I) קָוָה wait, await [qā/wâ'] 47

קוֹמָה height, stature [qô/må'] 46

(I) קָטֹן (adj.) small, young (-er, -est) [qā/ṭå'n] 47

קָשַׁב be sharp, attentive [qā/ša'b] 46

רָחַם* (Pi) show love for, have compassion on [rā/ḥa'm*] 47

רָצַח kill [rā/ṣa'ḥ] 47

שָׁבָה take captive [šā/bå'] 47

C. Words Occurring 45 and 44 Times (27)

(II) אוּלַי (adv.) perhaps ['û/la'i] 45

אֹכֶל food ['ō'/kel] 45

אֶשֶׁר* (pl.) fortune; happiness ['e'/šer*] 45

(II) בָּחוּר young man [bā/ḥû'r] 45

גִּיל* shriek ecstatically, shout with joy [gil*] 45

חָגַר gird, put on a belt [ḥā/ḡar] 44

חָלָב milk [ḥā/lāʹb] 44

חָלָץ take off; (Qal ptc. pass.) ready for battle [ḥā/laṣ] 44

יָרֵא (adj.) fearing, afraid of [yā/rēʹ] 45

יִרְאָה (n.) fear, reverence [yir/ʹâ] 45

מְדִינָה province, district [mədi/nâʹ] 45

מוֹשָׁב dwelling place [mô/šāʹb] 44

מָרָה be rebellious, obstinate [mā/râʹ] 45

מֶרְכָּבָה chariot [mer/kā/bâʹ] 44

(I) מַשָּׂא carrying, burden [maś/sāʹ] 45

נָגִיד chief, leader [nā/ḡîʹd] 44

נוֹרָא awe-inspiring [nô/rāʹ] 44

(I) נֵר lamp [nēr] 45

סָרִיס eunuch, court official [sā/rîʹs] 45

עוּד* (Pi) surround [ʿûdʹ] 45

עִמָּד* (alw. with suffix; prep.) with (cf. עִם, 1.B) [ʿim/mādʹ] 45

קָשַׁר tie up, bind [qā/šaʹr] 44

רוּעַ* (Hi) shout [rûʹaʿ] 44

רָפָה become slack; sink down [rā/p̄âʹ] 45

רֶשַׁע; רִשְׁעָה (s. m.; f.) wrong, injustice, guilt [reʹ/šaʿ; riš/ʿâʹ] 45

שֶׂה lamb, kid [śeh] 44

(I) שֶׁבֶר, שֵׁבֶר breaking, fracture; interpretation [šeʹ/ber, šēʹ/ber] 44

D. Words Occurring 43 and 42 Times (40)

אוֹר* shine [ʾôrʹ] 43

(I) אֱנוֹשׁ men [ʾĕnôʹš] 42

אֶפֶס (n.) end, nothingness; (particle of neg.; adv.) without [ʾe/p̄es] 42

(II) בַּד* (pl.) poles; shoots [badʹ] 42

בָּדַל* (Ni) separate oneself [bā/daʹl] 42

בָּזָה despise [bā/zâʹ] 43

בָּזַז (v.) plunder [bā/zaʹz] 42

(I) בֶּטַח safety; (adv.) securely [be/ṭaḥ] 43

בָּלַל moisten; confuse, confound [bā/laʹl] 43

גּוֹלָה exiles; deportation, exile [gô/lâʹ] 42

הָרָה conceive, become pregnant [hā/râʹ] 43

הָרַס demolish [hā/raʹs] 43

זוּב* (v.) flow; suffer a discharge [zûbʹ] 42

(I) זָמַר* (Pi) sing [zā/marʹ] 43

(I) זָרָה scatter [zā/râʹ] 42

חָרְבָּה desert, waste [ḥor/bâʹ] 42

טַף children [ṭap̄] 42

*יָחַל (Pi, Hi) wait [yā/ḥal'] 42

(I) יָסַד found, lay the foundations of [yā/sa'd] 43

(I)* יָסַר (Qal ptc.) teach; (Ni) teach oneself, take advice [yā/sa'r'] 42

יָתוֹם orphan [yā/tô'm] 42

כִּנּוֹר lyre [kin/nô'r] 42

לוּחַ tablet; board, plank [lú'aḥ] 43

מַחֲלֹקֶת portion, share [ma!/ḥălō'/qet] 42

מְנוֹרָה lampstand [mənô/rá'] 42

*מַעֲלָל (pl.) deed, act. [ma!/ʿălā'l'] 42

(I) מְעָרָה cave [mə'ā/rá'] 42

מָתַי (interr) when? [mā/ta'i] 43

נָוֶה pasturage, abode (I?); praiseworthy?, comely? (II?) [nā/we'h] 42

נִיחוֹחַ (adj.) soothing, tranquillizing [nî/ḥó'aḥ] 43

(I) נֵצַח luster, glory [nē'/ṣaḥ] 43

נָקִי (adj.) free from, exempt [nā/qi'] 43

נָתַץ tear down, demolish [nā/ta'ṣ] 42

פָּשַׁט take off [pā/ša'ṭ] 43

צַוָּאר neck [ṣaw/wā''r] 42

קִנְאָה passion [qin/'á'] 43

(I) רְחֹב, רְחוֹב broad open place, plaza [rəḥōb, rəḥôb] 43

(I) שָׁנִי crimson, scarlet [šā/ni'] 42

תְּבוּאָה (n.) produce, yield [təbû/'á'] 43

תְּבוּנָה intelligence, skill [təbû/ná'] 42

E. Words Occurring 41 and 40 Times (30)

(I) אַהֲבָה love ['a!/hăbá'] 40

(I)* אָזַן (Hi) listen (to) ['ā/za'n] 41

אָחוֹר back; (adv.) behind ['ā/ḥó'r] 41

(I) אָמֵץ be strong ['ā/ma'ṣ] 41

אָרַב lie in ambush ['ā/ra'b] 41

אֲשֵׁרָה Asherah; cult-post ['ăšē/rá'] 40

(I) בָּלַע (v.) swallow [bā/la'ʿ] 40

בְּרִיחַ bar [bərí'aḥ] 41

גָּבֹהַּ high [gā/bō'ah] 40

גַּן garden [gan] 41

דָּגָן grain [dā/ḡā'n] 40

דַּי sufficiency; enough [dai] 40

חָמַל feel compassion for [ḥā/ma'l] 41

חָרוֹן anger [ḥā/rṓ'n] 41

חָרַף (II) (v.) taunt, reproach [ḥā/ra/p̄] 40

יָפֶה (adj.) handsome, beautiful [yā/p̄e/h] 41

כָּבֵד (I) (n.; adj.) heavy, weighty; rich [kā/bē/d] 40

מוֹט* waver, reel, totter [mûṭ] 41

נוֹעַ* (v.) shake, totter [nú/a'] 41

נָחָה (v.) lead [nā/ḥá'] 40

נָטַשׁ leave, abandon [nā/ṭa/š] 40

נָקָה* (Ni) be free [nā/qā'] 41

עֹל yoke ['ōl] 40

פָּשַׁע (v.) revolt, rebel [pā/ša'] 41

צָדַק be in the right, have a just case [ṣā/da/q] 41

צִפּוֹר (I) (coll.) birds [ṣip/pó/r] 40

רָגַז (intrans.) shake, quake [rā/ḡa/z] 41

שֹׂנֵא enemy [śō/nē'] 41

שָׁקַט have peace, be at peace [šā/qa/ṭ] 41

תּוֹלֵעָה worm [tô/lē/'á'] 41

F. Words Occurring 39 and 38 Times (29)

אָבַל mourn ['ā/ba/l] 39

אֵיפָה ephah (grain measure) ['ê/p̄á'] 38

אָן; אָנָה (interr.) where? from where? ['ān; 'ā'/nâ] 38

אַרְגָּמָן purple ['ar/gā/mā/n] 39

בָּהַל* (Ni) be terrified [bā/ha/l] 39

גָּנַב steal [gā/na/b] 39

זַיִת olive (fruit and tree) [za'/yit] 38

חֶדֶר (dark) room, bedroom [ḥe/der] 38

חֵיק lap, bosom [ḥêq] 38

חֵפֶץ delight, joy [ḥē'/p̄eṣ] 39

חָרַד tremble, shudder [ḥā/ra/d] 39

חָרָשׁ craftsman [ḥā/rā/š] 38

כָּלַם* (Ni) be shamed, disgraced [kā/la/m] 38

מָטָר rain [mā/ṭā/r] 38

מְלֹא fulness, what fills [məlō'] 38

מִלָּה word, message [mil/lá'] 38

מַר (I) (adj.) bitter; (adv.) bitterly [mar] 39

מִרְמָה (I) deceit, fraud [mir/má'] 39

מָשִׁיחַ anointed (one) [mā/ší/aḥ] 39

מָשָׁל (I) saying, proverb [mā/šā/l] 39

פֹּעַל deed, work [pō/'a/l] 38

צֵלָע (I) rib [ṣē/lā'] 39

קָהַל* (Ni, intrans.) assemble [qā/haĺ] 39

רַחֲמִים compassion [ra!/ḥămîm] 39

(I) שַׁמָּה astonishment, horror [šam/mā́] 39

(III) שֵׁשׁ (Egyptian) linen [šēš] 38

תְּאֵנָה fig (-tree) [tə'ē/nā́] 39

תּוֹלְדוֹת descendants, genera-tions [tô/lē/dṓt] 39

תִּירוֹשׁ wine [tî/rṓš] 38

G. Words Occurring 37 and 36 Times (38)

(I) אִי coast, region ['î] 36

אָלָה (n.) curse ['ā/lā́] 37

אִמְרָה word, utterance ['im/rā́] 37

אָשֵׁם be(come) guilty ['ā/šám] 36

(I) בְּאֵר well, pit [bə'ḗr] 37

בִּינָה insight [bî/nā́] 37

גָּמַל finish; (Ni) be weaned [gā/mál] 37

חָסָה seek refuge [ḥā/sā́] 37

(I) חָרֵב (stat.) be dry [ḥā/rḗb] 36

טֻמְאָה (state of cultic) unclean-ness [ṭum/'ā́] 37

יָקָר (adj.) rare, costly; noble [yā/qā́r] 36

יֵשַׁע salvation, liberation [yē/ša'] 36

כּוֹכָב star [kô/kā́b] 37

כּוּל* seize; (Hi) contain; (Pilp) clasp [kûl] 37

כָּנַע* (Ni) be subdued, humbled [kā/na'] 36

כָּרַע bend the knee, kneel [kā/ra'] 36

לָקַט gather (up), glean [lā/qáṭ] 37

(I) מִבְצָר fortress, fortified city [mib/ṣā́r] 37

מוּל (n.) front; (as prep.) front of, towards [mûl] 36

מוֹפֵת sign, omen [mô/pḗt] 36

מָעוֹז fortress [mā/'ṓz] 36

מַצֵּבָה pillar [maṣ/ṣē/bā́] 36

מָשַׁךְ seize, pull [mā/šák] 36

(I) נוּף* (Hi) move back and forth [nûp] 36

נֵכָר foreign land [nē/kā́r] 36

נָסָה* (Pi) (put someone to the) test [nā/sā́] 36

(I) עֵדֶר flock, herd ['ē/der] 37

עֳנִי misery, affliction ['ŏnî] 36

עָשַׁק oppress, do wrong ['ā/šáq] 37

עֹשֶׁר riches ['ṓ/šer] 37

פִּלֶגֶשׁ; פִּילֶגֶשׁ concubine [pi!/le/ḡeš; pi/le/ḡeš] 37

(I) צָפָה keep guard, watch [ṣā/pā́] 37

קָשֶׁה (adj.) hard, severe [qā/šeʹh] 36

שָׂחַק play (act.) clumsy; laugh [śā/ḥaʹq] 36

שׁוֹעֵר gatekeeper [šó/ʿēʹr] 37

תֵּבֵל continent(s) [tē/bēʹl] 36

תְּהוֹם (n.) deep, ocean depths [təhóʹm] 36

תְּרוּעָה shout (of alarm, joy) [tərû/ʿâʹ] 36

H. Words Occurring 35 and 34 Times (41)

אוֹפַן wheel [ʾô/p̄aʹn] 35

אָרַךְ be long [ʾā/raʹk] 34

אָתוֹן she-ass [ʾā/tóʹn] 34

גֹּרֶן threshing floor [gōʹ/ren] 34

(I) גֶּשֶׁם rain [geʹ/šem] 35

דָּג; דָּגָה (m.; f. coll.) fish [dāḡ; dā/ḡâʹ] 34

(I) הַב Cf. יָהַב, 5.H [hab] 34

הָמָה make noise, roar [hā/mâʹ] 34

זֹנָה (female) prostitute [zō/nâʹ] 35

(I) זָרַק scatter [zā/raʹq] 34

חָבָא* (Ni) hide (oneself), be hidden [ḥā/bāʹʾ*] 34

חָזוֹן vision [ḥā/zóʹn] 35

חֵטְא fault, sin [ḥēṭʾ] 35

חָסִיד (one who is) faithful, devout [ḥā/síʹd] 35

יָהַב (impv.) give; (interj.) come on! [yā/haʹb] 34

יָנַק suck(le), nurse [yā/naʹq] 34

יָרֵךְ upper thigh [yā/rēʹk] 34

כָּכָה (adv.) so, thus [kā/kâʹ] 35

כַּלָּה daughter-in-law; bride [kal/lâʹ] 34

לְאֹם people [lə/ʾōm] 35

(I) מָחָה wipe off; wipe out [mā/ḥâʹ] 34

מַלְכָּה queen [mal/kâʹ] 35

מָעַל be unfaithful [mā/ʿaʹl] 35

מִשְׁנֶה second, double [miš/neʹh] 35

נָקַם take vengeance [nā/qaʹm] 35

סֵתֶר hiding place; garment [sēʹ/ter] 35

עֶבְרָה arrogance [ʿeb/râʹ] 34

עֵגֶל (bull-) calf [ʿēʹ/ḡel] 35

(I) עַם kinsman, relative [ʿam] 34

עָרֵל (adj.) uncircumcised [ʿā/rēʹl] 35

צָפַן (v.) hide; treasure up [ṣā/p̄aʹn] 34

צָרַעַת skin disease (not leprosy) [ṣā/ra/ʿat] 35

צָרַף smelt, refine [ṣā/raʹp̄] 34

קָנָא* (Pi) be envious of; arouse jealousy [qā/nāʹʾ] 34

59

קָצֶה end, border [qā/ṣā'] 35

קָצַף be(come) angry [qā/ ṣáp] 34

(I) קָצַר reap, harvest [qā/ṣár] 35

רָשַׁע be(come) guilty [rā/ šá'] 35

שְׂעֹרָה barley [śə'ō/rā'] 34

(II) תִּקְוָה expectation, hope [tiq/ wā'] 34

תְּשׁוּעָה salvation [təšû/'â'] 34

I. Words Occurring 33 and 32 Times (38)

אַרְמוֹן palace ['ar/mô'n] 33

(II) גְּדוּד raiding party [gədûd] 33

חָבַשׁ bind, bind on; saddle [ḥā/ba'š] 33

חִנָּם (adv.) without compensation; in vain [ḥin/nā'm] 32

חָתַן become related by marriage; (Qal ptc.) father- (mother-) in-law [ḥā/ta'n] 33

טַבָּח butcher, cook [ṭab/ bā'ḥ] 32

טוּב (n.) goodness, the best [ṭûb] 32

(I) יוֹנָה dove [yô/nā'] 33

יְמָנִי right (hand); southern [yəmā/ní'] 33

(I) יָרָה throw; shoot [yā/rā'] 33

כָּחַד* (Ni) be hidden [kā/ ḥa'd] 32

כֶּלֶב dog [ke'/leb] 32

לְבוּשׁ garment; (coll.) clothes [ləbûš] 32

מְאוּמָה anything (at all) [mə'û/ mā'] 32

(I) מוּל* circumcise [mûl'] 32

מִזְרָק sprinkling basin [miz/ rā'q] 32

מָחֳרָת (n.) the following day; (adv.) on the next day [mo!/ḥŏrā't] 32

מֵעֶה* (d. const.) bowels, abdomen [mē/'e'h'] 32

מַעֲשֵׂר tithe [ma!/'ăśē'r] 32

(I) נָשַׁק kiss [nā/šá'q] 32

עַוְלָה wickedness ['aw/lā'] 32

(I) עֻמָּה* (alw. pref. with ־לְ; adv.) just like; (prep.) close to, at ['um/mā''] 32

עֵרֶךְ layer, row; accessories ['ē'/rek] 33

עֹרֶף neck, nape ['ō'/rep̄] 33

עֵשֶׂב (coll.) green plants, herbs ['ē'/śeb] 33

פְּנִימִי (adj.) inner [pənî/mí'] 33

פְּקֻדָּה appointment, service [pəqud/dā'] 33

פָּרַח (I) sprout; break out [pā/raḥ] 32

צַד (I) side [ṣad] 33

צָמַח (v.) sprout [ṣā/maḥ] 33

קְלָלָה curse [qəlā/lá'] 33

רֶחֶם, רַחַם (II) womb [re'/ḥem, ra'/ḥam] 32

רִמּוֹן (I) pomegranate [rim/mô'n] 32

רִנָּה (I) shout of joy [rin/ná'] 33

שְׁבוּת; שְׁבִית (carrying off to) captivity, imprisonment [šəbût; šəbît] 32

שֹׁרֶשׁ root [šō'/reš] 33

תּוֹדָה (song, sacrifice of) thanksgiving [tô/dá'] 32

תַּחְתִּי; תַּחְתּוֹן (adj.) lower, lowest; (n.) the lowest [taḥ/tî'; taḥ/tô'n] 32

J. Words Occurring 31 Times (26)

אֵי (interr.) where? ['ê]

אֳנִיָּה ship ['oniy/yá']

אֶצְבַּע finger ['eṣ/ba'']

בְּכִי weeping [bəkî']

גָּג roof [gāḡ]

דָּמָה (I) be (a)like [dā/má']

חַלּוֹן window (-opening) [ḥal/lô'n]

טַל dew, light rain [ṭal]

טָמַן hide; set up secretly [ṭā/ma'n]

יָלַל* (Hi) howl, wail [yā/la'l]

כּוֹס (I) (drinking-) cup [kôs]

כָּזָב lie, falsehood [kā/zā'b]

כִּלְיָה* (pl.) kidney [kil/yá']

כְּפִיר young lion [kəpîr]

מִין kind, species [mîn]

נָאַף commit adultery [nā/'áp]

נָדַר make a vow [nā/da'r]

נָחָשׁ (I) serpent [nā/ḥā'š]

סֻכָּה thicket; hut [suk/ká']

עָב (II) cloud(s) ['āb]

עָצוּם (adj.) mighty, vast ['ā/ṣû'm]

פֶּסֶל idol [pe'/sel]

צוּר* (I) tie up, gather [ṣûr]

שִׂמְלָה mantle, wrapper (cf. שַׂלְמָה, 5.V) [śim/lá']

שְׁבוּעָה oath [šəbû/'á']

שָׁטַף wash away, wash off [šā/ṭa'p]

K. Words Occurring 30 and 29 Times (41)

בָּחַן test [bā/ḥa'n] 30

בַּמָּה, בַּמֶּה (interr. pron.) how? [bam/má'; bam/me'h] 29

בָּרָד hail [bā/rā'd] 29

בֶּשֶׂם; בֹּשֶׂם balsam shrub [bō'/śem; be'/śem] 30

בֹּשֶׁת shame [bōʹ/šet] 30

גָּזַל tear off, pull off, seize [gā/zaʹl] 30

הָדָר ornament [hā/dāʹr] 30

(I) זִמָּה plan; infamy [zim/māʹ] 29

חִטָּה wheat [ḥiṭ/ṭāʹ] 30

חָמַם be(come) warm, hot [ḥā/maʹm] 29

חֲצֹצְרָה trumpet [ḥăṣō/ṣərāʹ] 29

(I) חֵרֶם ban, (what is) banned [ḥēʹ/rem] 29

חָשַׂךְ restrain, withhold [ḥā/śaʹk] 29

יָעַד designate [yā/ʿaʹd] 29

כְּלִמָּה (n.) disgrace, insult [kəlim/māʹ] 30

כֻּתֹּנֶת tunic [kut/tōʹ/net] 29

(I) לָבָן (adj.) white [lā/bāʹn] 29

מַאֲכָל food; fodder [ma!/ʾăkāʹl] 30

מִטָּה bed, couch [miṭ/ṭāʹ] 29

מָנָה (v.) count [mā/nāʹ] 29

מָנַע retain, withhold [mā/naʹʿ] 29

(I) מַעַל unfaithfulness [maʹ/ʿal] 29

נִדָּה; נִדָה menstrual flow; excretion [nid/dāʹ; nî/dāʹ] 30

נָהַג* drive, lead [nā/haʹḡ] 30

סִיר (cooking-) pot [sîr] 30

סָפַד mourn, sound a lament [sā/pāʹd] 30

עָלַם (Qal ptc.) secret (faults); (Ni) be hidden [ʿā/laʹm] 29

עִשָּׂרוֹן tenth part [ʿiś/śā/rôʹn] 30

עַתּוּד* (pl.) ram, he-goat; (met.) leader [ʿat/tûʹdˣ] 29

פִּנָּה corner [pin/nāʹ] 30

פָּרָה bear fruit [pā/rāʹ] 29

(I) קֶצֶף anger, rage [qeʹ/ṣep] 29

קִרְיָה city, town [qir/yāʹ] 30

רָבַץ lie down, crouch [rā/baʹṣ] 30

(I) רָעַשׁ quake, shake [rā/ʿaʹš] 30

שֵׂעָר (coll.) hair [śē/ʿāʹr] 29

(I) שָׂרִיד survivor [śā/rîʹd] 29

שְׁמִינִי (ord.) eighth [šəmî/nîʹ] 30

שָׁפֵל (stat.) be low, sink [šā/pēʹl] 29

שִׁקּוּץ abominable idol; abomination [šiq/qûʹṣ] 29

תְּנוּפָה waving, shaking; (ext.) wave-offering [tənû/pāʹ] 30

L. Words Occurring 28 and 27 times (54)

אַדִּיר (adj.) mighty; (n., pl.) nobles [ʾad/dîr] 27

אָוָה* (Ni?) be beautiful, lovely; (Pi) want, crave [ʾā/wâʾʾ] 27

(I) אֱוִיל (adj.) foolish; (n.) fool, simpleton [ʾĕwîl] 27

בַּז (n.) plunder (act and objects of) [baz] 27

בְּלִיַּעַל wickedness [bəliy/ya/ʿal] 27

בָּשַׁל ripen, cook; (Pi) cook, boil [bā/šal] 28

זָקֵן (stat.) be old [zā/qēʾn] 27

(II) חָבַר become allies, unite [ḥā/bar] 28

חָכַם be(come) wise [ḥā/kam] 27

חָלַם be(come) strong; (Qal, Hi) dream [ḥā/lam] 28

(I) חָלַף pass by, follow each other [ḥā/lap] 27

חֲמִישִׁי (ord.) fifth; (fract.) one-fifth [ḥămî/šîʾ] 27

חָקַר spy out, investigate [ḥā/qar] 27

חָתַם seal up, confirm [ḥā/tam] 27

יוֹבֵל ram; year of jubilee [yô/bēʾl] 27

יָצַת kindle, burn up [yā/ṣat] 27

יָרֵחַ moon [yā/rēʾaḥ] 27

יְרֵכָה rear, back side [yərē/kâ] 28

יָשַׁר be (go) straight [yā/šar] 27

כַּפֹּרֶת (performance of) reconciliation; (trad.) cover, lid [kap/pōʾ/ret] 27

לִיץ* boast; (Hi) mock, be a spokesman (interpreter) [lîṣʾ] 28

מָבוֹא; מוֹבָא entrance [mā/bôʾ; mô/bāʾ] 27

(I) מוֹצָא outlet; what comes out [mô/ṣāʾ] 27

מוֹקֵשׁ trap [mô/qēʾš] 27

מוֹשִׁיעַ helper, deliverer [mô/šîʾaʿ] 27

(II) מֶלַח salt [meʾ/laḥ] 28

מְסִלָּה road, highway [məsil/lâ] 27

מְעִיל robe [məʿîl] 28

(II) נֵבֶל, נְבֶל harp? [nēʾ/bel, neʾ/bel] 27

נְדָבָה free will; voluntary gift [nədā/bâ] 27

נָדַד flee, wander [nā/dad] 27

נָדִיב willing; (one who is) noble [nā/dī'b] 27

נוּד* wander [nûd'] 27

נְקָמָה vengeance, revenge [nəqā/mā'] 27

נָתַק tear away, draw (one) away [nā/taq'] 27

עוּף* (I) fly; (Pol) soar; (Hithpol) fly off ['ûp'] 27

עֲשִׂירִי (ord.) tenth; (fract.) one-tenth ['ăśî/rî'] 28

פֶּחָה governor [pe!/ḥā'] 28

פָּלַט escape [pā/laṭ'] 27

פְּלֵיטָה (n.) escape [pəlê/ṭā'] 28

פָּתָה (I) be inexperienced, naïve [pā/tā'] 28

קָרָה happen, come about [qā/rā'] 27

קָשָׁה be hard, heavy [qā/šā'] 28

רְכוּשׁ property, goods [rəkûš] 28

שׂוּשׂ* rejoice [śûś'] 27

שָׂטָן accuser, adversary; the Satan [śā/ṭā'n] 27

שָׂכָר (I) wages, reward [śā/kā'r] 28

שִׁטָּה acacia (tree, wood) [šiṭ/ṭā'] 28

שָׁלֵם (I) (adj.) uninjured, safe; complete [šā/lē'm] 28

שְׁמוּעָה news, report [šəmû/'ā'] 27

שִׁשִּׁי (ord.) sixth; (fract.) one-sixth [šiš/šî'] 27

תֵּבָה ark, chest [tē/bā'] 28

תָּלָה hang [tā/lā'] 27

תֹּם integrity, completeness [tōm] 28

M. Words Occurring 26 and 25 Times (53)

אִוֶּלֶת foolishness ['iw/wi'/let] 25

אֵיפֹה (interr.) where? ['ê/pō'h] 25

אָמֵן (interj.) amen! surely! ['ā/mē'n] 25

אָפָה bake ['ā/pā'] 25

אֵפוֹא (adv.) then, so ['ē/pô'] 25

בָּצוּר (Qal ptc. pass.) impregnable [bā/ṣû'r] 25

בֶּרֶךְ knee [be'/rek] 25

גָּבַר excel; (Hi) be strong [gā/ba'r] 25

דְּמוּת likeness [dəmût] 25

הָגָה (I) mutter, growl [hā/ḡā'] 25

הוֹן wealth [hôn] 26

חִיצוֹן (adj.) outer [ḥî/ṣō'n] 25

חָצֵב quarry, hew (out), stir? (II?) [ḥā/ṣē'b] 25

חָרַשׁ (I) plow; engrave [ḥā/ra'š] 25

חֹשֶׁן breast-plate (of the high priest) [ḥō'/šen] 25

טוּר row, course (of building stone) [ṭûr] 26

טָרַף tear in pieces [tā/ra'p̄] 25

יָגַע grow weary [yā/ḡa'ʿ] 26

(I) יָשֵׁן go to sleep; sleep [yā/ša'n] 25

כַּעַס, כַּעַשׂ irritation, anger [ka'/ʿas, ka'/ʿaś] 25

מַגֵּפָה plague, torment [mag/gē/p̄ā'] 26

מְכוֹנָה place, abode; stand [məkô/nā'] 25

מָסָךְ covering, curtain [mā/sā'k] 25

(I) מַסֵּכָה cast image; drink offering [mas/sē/kā'] 26

מָצוֹר affliction (I?); fortification (II?) [mā/ṣô'r] 25

מָרַד (v.) rebel [mā/ra'd] 25

נֵזֶר consecration (of the Nazirite) [nē'/zer] 25

נֹכַח (prep.) in front of, opposite; (n.) what lies opposite [nō'/kaḥ] 25

נֶשֶׁר eagle, vulture [ne'/šer] 26

נָתִיב; נְתִיבָה (s. m.; f.) path [nā/tîb; nəti/bā'] 26

(I) סוּג* deviate, be disloyal [sûḡ*] 25

(III) סַף threshhold [sap] 25

עֲגָלָה wagon, cart [ʿăḡā/lā'] 25

עִוֵּר (adj.) blind [ʿiw/wē'r] 26

עֲלִילָה deed, action [ʿălî/lā'] 25

(I) עָשָׁן smoke [ʿā/šā'n] 25

(I) פַּח bird, trap [paḥ] 25

פָּחַד tremble [pā/ḥa'd] 25

פָּרַד (Qal ptc. pass.) outspread; (Ni) divide, (intrans.) separate [pā/ra'd] 26

פָּרֹכֶת curtain [pā/rō'/ket] 25

פִּתְאֹם (adv.) suddenly [pit/ʾō'm] 25

צוֹם (act, time of) fasting [ṣôm] 25

קָדַם* (Pi) be in front, walk at the head [qā/da'm*] 26

רָגַל slander; (Pi) spy out; (Tifel unc.) teach (someone) to walk [rā/ḡa'l] 26

(I) רָדָה tread (winepress); rule [rā/dā'] 25

רָחַב open wide, broaden [rā/ḥa'b] 25

שְׁאָר remainder, remnant [šə'ʾār] 26

(II) שֹׁד violence, destruction [šōd] 25

שֹׁטֵר officer, recordkeeper [šō/ṭē'r] 25

שָׁלַף draw (sword); take off [šā/la'p̄] 25

שִׁלְשׁוֹם (idiom.) three (days ago, day before yesterday) [šil/šô'm] 25

תּוּר* go about, explore; (ext.) spy out [ṭûr˝] 25

תִּחְנָּה (I) supplication (for mercy); pardon, mercy [təḥin/nâ'] 25

N. Words Occurring 24 Times (30)

אֵבֶל (rites of) mourning [ʾē'/bel]

אוֹי (interj.) woe!; (n.) woe [ʾôy]

אֵיד disaster, calamity [ʾêd]

אַרְבֶּה locust [ʾar/beʰ]

בִּשֵּׂר* (Pi) bring news [bā/śaŕ˝]

גָּוַע expire, die, perish [gā/waʿ]

דִּין* (v.) judge; bring justice [dîn˝]

הוֹד (I) height, majesty [hôd]

זִכָּרוֹן reminder [zik/kā/rô'n]

חוּס* pity, be troubled about [ḥûs˝]

חֳלִי illness, suffering [ḥŏlî]

חֶלְקָה (II) piece of land, plot of ground [ḥel/qâ']

יָתֵד peg, tent-peg [yā/tē'd]

כָּבָה be extinguished [kā/bâ']

כֹּתֶרֶת (column-) capital [kō/te'/ret]

מְלוּכָה kingship [məlû/kâ']

נָאַץ reject, disdain [nā/ʾaʿṣ]

נָזָה be sprinkled; (intrans.) spatter [nā/zâ']

נָסַךְ (I) pour out [nā/saʿk]

נְשָׁמָה blowing; breath [nəšā/mâ']

סַעַר; סְעָרָה (s. m.; f.) gale, windstorm [sa/ʿar; sə/ʿā/rấ']

פָּלִיט, פָּלֵיט fugitive(s.) [pā/lîṭ, pā/lê'ṭ]

פִּקּוּדִים directions, orders [piq/qû/dî'm]

רָבַב (I) be(come) great, much, numerous [rā/baʿb]

רוּשׁ* be poor [rûš˝]

שַׁחַר dawn [ša/ḥar]

שָׁכֹל (stat.) be bereaved (of children) [šā/kō'l]

שָׁנָה (v.) change; repeat [šā/nâ']

תּוֹכַחַת reprimand [tô/ka/ḥat]

תֵּימָן (I) south; southern area [tê/mā'n]

O. Words Occurring 23 Times (35)

אָבִיר, אַבִּיר strong, powerful [ʾā/bîr, ʾab/bîr]

בַּד (III) linen [bad]

בֶּצַע a piece cut off [be'/ṣaʿ]

גָּלַח* (Pi) shave [gā/laʿḥ˝]

דִּמְעָה (s. coll.) tears [dim/ʿâ']

זֵכֶר mention, remembrance [zē'/ker]

(I) חוֹל sand, mud [ḥôl]

חָסֵר (stat.) lack, be lacking; diminish [ḥā/sē'r]

(I) חָפַר dig [ḥā/pā'r]

חָפַשׂ search out, check [ḥā/pā'ś]

יָעַל* (Hi) help, be of use [yā/ʿa'l*]

(I) יִצְהָר olive oil [yiṣ/hā'r]

כָּהַן* (Pi) perform the duties of priest [kā/ha'n*]

כִּיּוֹר (wash-) basin, pot [kiy/yô'r]

(I) מָדוֹן; מִדְיָן quarrel, dispute [mā/dô'n; mid/yā'n]

מִישׁוֹר level ground, plain [mî/šô'r]

מַס compulsary labor, corvée [mas]

מַעְיָן spring [maʿ/yā'n]

מִקְרָא convocation [miq/rā']

מְרִי obstinacy [mərî]

נָגַשׂ beat, drive [nā/ḡa'ś]

נָקַב pierce; designate [nā/qa'b]

(I) סָכַךְ isolate, cover [sā/ka'k]

עַז (adj.) defiant, shameless [ʿaz]

(I) עֲטָרָה wreath, crown [ʿăṭā/rā']

עָשִׁיר (adj.) wealthy, rich [ʿā/šî'r]

פָּסִיל* (pl.) idols [pā/sî'l*]

צָהֳרַיִם (d.) midday, noon [ṣo!/hŏra'/yim]

שֹׁחַד gift; bribe [šō'/ḥad]

שַׁחַת pit(-fall), grave [ša'/ḥat]

שֵׁכָר intoxicating drink, beer? [šē/kā'r]

שֵׁנָה sleep [šē/nā']

תּוֹצָאוֹת (pl.) exits; starting point [tô/ṣā/'ô't]

תְּחִלָּה beginning [təḥil/lā']

תְּמוֹל yesterday [təmôl]

P. Words Occurring 22 Times (37)

(III) אַיִל gatepost? [ʾa'/yil]

אַיָּל; אַיָּלָה fallow deer (buck; doe) [ʾay/yā'l; ʾay/yā/lā']

אֵפֶר ashes, dust [ʾē'/per]

גָּדַע cut off [gā/da'ʿ]

(I) דָּמַם stand (keep) still [dā/ma'm]

דָּת regulation, law [dāt]

הִין hin (liquid measure) [hîn]

(II) זָהַר* (Ni) be warned; (Hi) warn [zā/ha'r*]

זַעַם (n.) curse [za'/ʿam]

טֶרֶף prey; food [ṭe'/rep]

יוֹעֵץ counsellor [yô/ʿē'ṣ]

כָּחַשׁ become lean; (Pi) deny, deceive [kā/ḥa'š]

כָּלָה destruction, annihilation [kā/lā']

לוּ, לוּא (imprec.) if only; O that … might [lû, lû']

מוֹלֶדֶת descendants, kindred [mô/le'/det]

מַחְתָּה fire-pan [maḥ/tâ']

מָעַט be(come) few [mā/ʿaṭ]

נַעַל sandal [na'/ʿal]

נָפַץ smash; scatter (II?); (Ni) break up [nā/p̄áṣ]

נְקֵבָה (n., adj.) female [nəqē/bâ']

סָקַל (v.) stone [sā/qal]

עֲבֹת rope ['ābōt]

פֶּגֶר corpse [pe'/ḡer]

פָּשָׂה (v.) spread [pā/śā']

(I) צָעִיר small(-er, -est); young (-er, -est) [ṣā/ʿî'r]

קִיץ* spend the summer [qîṣ*]

רֶגַע tranquillity; moment [re'/ḡaʿ]

רֶשֶׁת (bird) net [re'/šet]

שָׂשׂוֹן joy [śā/śô'n]

שָׁוַע* (Pi) cry for help [šā/waʿ*]

שָׁזַר* (Ho ptc.) twisted [šā/zar*]

(I) שְׁכֶם shoulder(s) [šəkem]

שָׁעַן* (Ni) lean (against); (met.) depend (on) [šā/ʿa'n*]

שָׁקַל weigh (out) [šā/qal]

שָׁקַף* (Ni, Hi) look down [šā/qap̄*]

תַּזְנוּת obscene manner [taz/nû't]

תָּעַב* (Ni) be loathed, abhorrent [tā/ʿab*]

Q. Words Occurring 21 Times (40)

אָתָה come ['ā/tâ']

בְּעוֹד while yet, as long as (cf. עוֹד, 2.A) [bə/ʿôd]

(I) בָּרָק lightning [bā/rā'q]

(I) גָּרַע shave; diminish [gā/raʿ]

(II) זָנַח reject [zā/naḥ]

(I) חוּשׁ* hurry [ḥûš*]

חָמַד desire, crave [ḥā/mad]

חֹתֵן father-in-law [ḥō/tē'n]

לָבֹנָה, לְבוֹנָה frankincense [lā/bō/nâ', ləbô/nâ']

(I) לְחִי chin, jawbone [ləḥî']

מְגִלָּה scroll [məḡil/lā']

מוּם, מְאוּם blemish [mûm, mə'ûm]

מְנוּחָה rest, resting place [mənû/ḥâ']

מָסַס lose courage; (Ni) dissolve [mā/sás]

(II) מַשָּׂא utterance [maś/śā'']

(I) מִשְׁחָה anointing [miš/ḥâ']

מַשְׁקֶה cup-bearer; well-irrigated land [maš/qe'h]

מֹת* (?) (pl.) men [mōt⁺]

נֵס signal pole; banner [nēs]

נָתַךְ gush forth, be poured out [nā/ta´k]

נָתַשׁ uproot, tear out [nā/ta´ś]

סוֹד confidential conversation [sôd]

סָחַר pass through, wander around [sā/ḥa´r]

סָפָה take away [sā/pá´]

סֶרֶן* (II) (pl.) prince [se´/ren⁺]

עָוֶל wrong, injustice [ʿā´/wel]

עָנָו (K; adj.) humble [ʿā/ nā´w]

פָּקַח (v.) open [pā/qa´ḥ]

פַּרְסָה (divided) hoof [par/sá´]

צוּם* (v.) fast [ṣûm⁺]

צְעָקָה (n.) cry, call for help [ṣə´ā/qá´]

רָחָב (I) (adj.) wide, broad [rā/ ḥab]

שָׂמֵחַ (adj.) joyful, glad [śā/ mē´aḥ]

שָׁאַג (v.) roar [šā/ʾa´g̱]

שָׁבַר (II) buy (food) [šā/ba´r]

שָׁגָה stray, go astray [šā/g̱á´]

שַׁד* (d.) breast [šad⁺]

שַׁחַק (coll.) dust; clouds of dust? [ša´/ḥaq]

תַּאֲוָה longing, desire [ta!/ʾăwá´]

תָּמַךְ grasp [tā/ma´k]

R. Words Occurring 20 Times (33)

אֱלִיל worthless; (ext.) pagan gods [ʾĕlíl]

בִּקְעָה plain, broad valley [biq/ ʿá´]

בְּרוֹשׁ (Phoenician) juniper [bərôš]

גַּל (I) heap [gal]

חָבַל (I) take (something) in pledge [ḥā/ba´l]

חָלִיל (II) (neg. interj.) be it far from [ḥā/lí´l]

חָתָן son-in-law; bridegroom [ḥā/tā´n]

יָחַשׂ* (Hith) be enrolled (in genealogical registry) [yā/ḥa´ś⁺]

יָנָה* be violent, oppress; (Hi) oppress [yā/ná⁺]

יְסוֹד foundation(-wall), base [yəsôd]

מְהֵרָה (n.) speed, haste; (adv.) quickly [məhē/rá´]

מוּשׁ* (II) withdraw; (Hi) remove [mûš⁺]

מְזוּזָה doorpost [məzû/zá´]

מַחְסֶה refuge [maḥ/se´h]

מִקְלָט refuge, asylum [miq/lā´ṭ]

מִשְׁמָר guard [miš/mā´r]

עֲלִיָּה upper room, roof-chamber [ʿăliy/yá´]

עָמָל labor, exert oneself [ʿā/ ma´l]

עָרִיץ (adj.) violent, mighty; (n.) master [ˁā/rîṣ]

עָתַר (I) pray; (Ni) be moved by entreaties [ˁā/tar]

צִנָּה (II) shield [ṣin/nā']

צַר (I) (adj.) narrow; (n.) distress [ṣar]

צָרַע* (Qal, Pu ptc.) suffering from a skin disease [ṣā/raˁ]

קַיִץ summer; summer fruit [qa/yiṣ]

קָסַם practice divination [qā/sam]

שָׂגַב be (too) high; be fortified [śā/ḡab]

שֵׂיב; שֵׂיבָה old age [śêb; śê/bā']

שִׂיחַ be(come) concerned, consider [śî/aḥ]

שָׁבוּעַ week [šā/bú/aˁ]

שָׁכֵן inhabitant, neighbor [šā/kēn]

שְׁפֵלָה the lowland(s) [šə/pē/lā']

תַּבְנִית shape, form; pattern [tab/nît]

תֹּהוּ wasteland, formlessness; nothingness [tō/hû]

S. Words Occurring 19 Times (41)

אוּלָם (I) (advs.) on the other hand, however [ʾú/lā'm]

אָפִיק (I) stream-channel [ʾā/pî'q]

אַשְׁמָה guilt [ʾaš/mā']

בָּרַר purge out, sort; sharpen? (II?) [bā/rar]

גַּאֲוָה loftiness; haughtiness [ga!/ʾăwā']

גְּמוּל doings; recompense [gəmûl]

דִּין lawsuit [dîn]

זָקָן beard [zā/qā'n]

חַטָּא sinner; sinful [ḥaṭ/ṭā']

חָקַק hew out; engrave [ḥā/qaq]

יָאַל* (II) (Hi) make a beginning [yā/ʾa'l]

יֳפִי beauty [yŏpî]

לָאָה be(come) weary [lā/ʾā']

לֶהָבָה flame [le!/hā/bā']

לָחַץ crowd, press; oppress [lā/ḥaṣ]

מָאוֹר luminary [mā/ʾô'r]

מְזִמָּה plan, plot [məzim/mā']

מֵישָׁרִים straightness, fairness [mê/šā/rî'm]

מַעֲלָה ascent, steep path [ma!/ˁăle'h]

מַעֲרָכָה row; battle line [ma!/ˁărā/kā']

נָבֵל (I) wither [nā/bē'l]

נֹגַהּ (I) brightness, shining [nō'/ḡah]

עָלֶה leaves, leaf [ˁā/le'h]

עֵנָב grape (cluster) ['ē/nā'b]

עַשְׁתֵּי (f.) eleven(th) ['aš/té']

(I) פֶּרֶץ breach, gap [pē'/res]

(I) פֶּתִי (adj.) young, naïve [pe'/tî]

רִיק* (v.) empty out, draw (sword); muster [rîq*]

רָמַס trample, tread [rā/ma's]

רֹעַ bad quality [rō'a']

רָעֵב (adj.) hungry [rā/'ē'b]

רַעֲנָן (adj.) luxuriant [ra!/'ănā'n]

רָצַץ smash up; abuse [rā/ṣa's]

שָׂכַר hire [śā/ka'r]

שָׁאַב draw (water) [šā/'a'b]

שְׁגָגָה error, inadvertence [šə/ḡā/ḡā']

שׁוֹק thigh; (ext.) leg [šôq]

שָׁכַר be(come) drunk(en) [šā/ka'r]

(I) שֶׁלֶג snow [še'/leḡ]

שָׁפָל (adj.) deep, low; humble [šā/pā'l]

תִּמֹרָה ornament of palm tree [ti!/mō/rā']

T. Words Occurring 18 Times (43)

(I) אוֹן power, strength, wealth ['ôn]

אָחַר delay, keep back ['ā/ḥa'r]

אָכְלָה food ['ok/lā']

אָכֵן (interj.) truly! indeed! ['ā/kē'n]

אֹרֵב ambush ['ō/rē'b]

בִּירָה citadel [bî/rā']

גַּחֶלֶת live coals [ga!/ḥe'/let]

דָּכָא* (Ni ptc.) oppressed; (Pi) crush [dā/kā'*]

זְעָקָה cry, call for help [zə'ā/qā']

זָרַח go forth, shine [zā/ra'ḥ]

חֵךְ palate [ḥēk]

חָסֵר (one who) lacks [ḥā/sē'r]

(I) חָצִיר grass [ḥā/ṣî'r]

חָשַׁךְ be (grow) dark [ḥā/ša'k]

יָבַל* (Hi) bring [yā/ba'l*]

כַּד jar [kad]

(I) כָּלָא restrain [kā/lā'*]

(II) כַּפְתּוֹר knob [kap/tô'r]

(I) לוּן* (Ni) murmur, grumble [lûn*]

לָעַג (v.) ridicule [lā/'a'ḡ]

מַטָּה (adv.) below, beneath [ma't/ṭâ]

מָעוֹן lair; dwelling [mā/'ô'n]

(II) מְצוּדָה mountain stronghold [məṣû/dā']

מָקוֹר spring, source [mā/qô'r]

מַקֵּל shoot, twig [maq/qē'l]

מֶרְחָק distance [mer/ḥā'q]

נָבָל (I) (adj.) foolish [nā/bā'l]

נָזַל trickle, flow; (Qal ptc. act.) brook, watercourse [nā/zal]

נָטַף drip [nā/ṭap̄]

סוּת* (Hi) lead astray, seduce [sût⁼]

סָרַר be stubborn (I?) [sā/ra'r]

עָטָה (v.) wrap, cover ['ā/ṭā']

עָלַל* (I) (Po) treat, deal with ['ā/lal⁼]

עָצַם (I) be mighty; numerous ['ā/ṣa'm]

צְבִי (I) ornament; glory [ṣəbî]

צַלְמָוֶת darkness [ṣal/mā'/wet]

קִינָה (I) dirge, lament [qî/nā']

רָכַל* (Qal ptc.) trader, merchant [rā/kal⁼]

שָׂכִיר (adj.) rented, hired; (n.) hired laborer, mercenary [śā/kî'r]

שָׁחַח stoop, crouch [šā/ḥa'ḥ]

שָׁקַד (I) be awake, watch [šā/qa'd]

תַּחֲנוּן* supplication [ta!/ḥănû'n⁼]

תָּכַן examine [tā/ka'n]

U. Words Occurring 17 Times (64)

אֶזְרָח native, citizen ['ez/rā'ḥ]

אֵימָה terror, dread ['ê/mā']

אָסִיר; אַסִּיר prisoner ['ā/sî'r; 'as/sî'r]

בָּאַשׁ stink [bā/'a'š]

בִּכּוּרִים first fruits [bik/kû/rî'm]

בְּרֵכָה pond, pool [bərē/kā']

גֹּבַהּ height [gō'/bāh]

גְּבִיר; גְּבִירָה (s. m.) lord, master; (f.) lady, mistress [gəbî'r; gəbî/rā']

גַּנָּב thief [gan/nā'b]

דָּמָה (II) come to rest, end; (Ni ext.?) be silent, destroy-ed (III?) [dā/mā']

דָּרוֹם south; south wind [dā/rô'm]

חֹזֶה vision [ḥō/ze'ḥ]

חִידָה riddle [ḥî/dā']

חֹמֶר (II) mortar, cement; clay [ḥō'/mer]

חָפֵר (II) (stat.) be ashamed [ḥā/pē'r]

חָפְשִׁי (adj.) freed, free [ḥop̄/šî']

חֶרֶשׂ clay, pottery [ḥe'/reś]

יוֹצֵר potter, founder [yô/ṣē'r]

יְקָר preciousness; honoring, esteeming [yəqā'r]

כֵּן stand, base; place (IV?); (ext.) position (V?) [kēn]

כְּתָב (n.) document; register [kətāb]

כָּתַת beat fine, pound up [kā/ta't]

מוּג* reel, melt [mûḡ*]

מָטַר* (Ni) be rained on; (Hi) have (make) rain fall [mā/ṭar*]

מָכוֹן place; support [mā/kôn]

מֶמְשָׁלָה dominion [mem/šā/lā́]

מַסְגֵּרֶת dungeon [mis/ge/ret]

מִשְׂגָּב high spot, refuge [miś/gā́b]

מָשׂוֹשׂ joy [mā/śôś]

מָשַׁל (I) make up (say) a (mocking-) verse [mā/šal]

מִשְׁעָן, מַשְׁעֵן; מַשְׁעֵנָה, מִשְׁעֶנֶת (m.; f.) support [miš/ʿān, maš/ʿēn; maš/ʿē/nā́, miš/ʿe/net]

מַתָּנָה (I) gift, present [mat/tā/nā́]

נָדַב urge on, prompt; (Hithp) volunteer [nā/dab]

נֶזֶם ring [ne/zem]

נָקָם (human) revenge; (divine) recompense [nā/qā́m]

נָקַף (II) make a (yearly) round [nā/qap̄]

נְתִין* (pl.) temple slave; bondsman [nā/tîn*]

סֶגֶן*, סָגָן (pl.) governor, prefect [se/ḡen*, sā/ḡā́n*]

עָוָה do wrong [ʿā/wā́]

עָיֵף (adj.) weary, faint [ʿā/yēp̄]

עָלַז exult [ʿā/laz]

עָמֹק (adj.) deep; (ext.) impenetrable [ʿā/mṓq]

עָצָב* (pl.) images, idols [ʿā/ṣā́b*]

עָרַב (I) stand (as) surety (for) [ʿā/rab]

עָשַׁר be(come) rich; (Hi) make someone rich [ʿā/šar]

פֶּרַח bud, flower [pe/raḥ]

צָמָא (n.) thirst [ṣā/mā́]

קָדַר grow dark, turbid [qā/dar]

קָלוֹן shame [qā/lô/n]

קְעָרָה dish [qə/ʿā/rā́]

רָמַשׂ swarm, teem [rā/maś]

רֶמֶשׂ (coll.) small animals, reptiles [re/meś]

רַעַשׁ quaking, commotion [ra/ʿaš]

רָקִיעַ plate; (met.) firmament [rā/qîʿaʿ]

שְׂבָכָה net; lattice, grille [śə bā/kā́]

שִׂנְאָה hate, hatred [śin/ʾā́]

שָׁאוֹן (II) din, uproar [šā/ʾô/n]

שְׁאֵר flesh, food; blood-relation [šə·ʾēr]

שׁוּשַׁן (I) lily, lotus [šû/ša/n]

שָׁלִישׁ (III) third man in chariot; (ext.) adjutant [šā/li/š]

שֵׁמַע hearsay, report [šē/maʿ]

תֶּבֶן straw, chaff [te/ben]

תֹּף timbrel, tambourine [tō/p̄]

תְּשִׁיעִי (ord.) ninth [tə ši/ʿî́]

V. Words Occurring 16 Times (64)

אוֹב (II) spirit (of the dead) [ʾôb]

אָזַר put on, gird [ʾā/zaŕ]

אֵיכָה (interr.) how? in what way? (cf. אֵיךְ, 4.H) [ʾê/kấ]

אֵלָה (I) mighty tree [ʾē/lấ]

אָמַל* (I) (Pul) dry up [ʾā/maĺ]

אָמְנָה; אָמְנָם, אֻמְנָם (adv.) truly, surely; (with interr.) really? [ʾom/nấ; ʾom/nā`m, ʾum/nāʹm]

בֹּהֶן* thumb; big toe [bō/hen˝]

בָּלָה become old and worn out [bā/lấ]

בַּלְעֲדֵי* (prep.) apart from, except for [bal/ˁădê˝]

בָּעַל (I) rule, own; marry [bā/ˁaĺ]

בָּעַת* (Ni) be terrified [bā/ˁaẗ]

בָּצַע cut off [bā/ṣaˁ]

גְּדִי kid (goat) [gədî]

גַּל* (II) (pl.) wave [gaĺ]

גַּנָּה garden [gan/nấ]

דְּבִיר (I) holy of holies [dəbîr]

דּוּשׁ* trample; thresh [dûš˝]

הָרָה (adj.) pregnant [hā/reˊh]

זוּלָה (prep.) except, besides; (conj.) except that [zû/lấ]

חָגַג celebrate [ḥā/ḡaḡ]

חֶמְדָּה something desirable, excellent [ḥem/dấ]

חֹרֶב dryness, drought; desolation [ḥō/reb]

חָשָׁה be quiet [ḥā/šấ]

טָבַל dip [ṭā/baĺ]

יְגִיעַ labor, work; gain [yəḡîˊaˁ]

יָצַג* (Hi) set (down), place [yā/ṣāḡ˝]

יֶקֶב wine-vat; winepress [ye/qeb]

כָּזַב lie; (Ni) prove to be a liar [kā/zaˊb]

לָבוּשׁ (adj.) clothed, dressed [lā/bûˊš]

לֵץ babbler, scoffer [lēṣ]

מַחֲצִית half [ma!/ḥăṣîˊt]

מַטָּרָה target; (men on) guard [maṭ/ṭā/rấ]

מַכְאֹב pain [mak/ʾōˊb]

מִכְסֶה cover(ing) [mik/seˊh]

מִסְפֵּד mourning (rites) [mis/pēˊd]

מָרַר be bitter [mā/raˊr]

מַשָּׂאָה; מַשְׂאֵת lifting up [maś/śā/ʾấ; maś/ʾēˊt]

נָזִיר (adj.) dedicated; (n.) Nazirite [nā/zîˊr]

נָשָׁא (I) lend, make a loan [nā/šāˊ]

נָשָׁא (II)* (Ni) be deceived [nā/šāʾʾ]

נָשָׁה (II) Cf. (I) נָשָׁא [nā/šá']

סוּפָה (I) (storm-) wind [sû/pấ']

סֹחֵר trader, merchant [sō/ḥēʾr]

סַם* (pl. coll.) perfume [samʾ]

עָנָה (IV) sing ['ā/nā']

עָרוֹם (adj.) naked ['ā/rôʾm]

עָרְלָה foreskin ['or/lá']

פָּרַע let (hang) loose [pā/raʿ]

פֵּשֶׁת flax, linen [pēʾ/šet]

צוּד* hunt [ṣûdʾ]

צִיָּה dry country, desert [ṣiy/yáʾ]

צֶמֶר wool [ṣeʾ/mer]

קֶלַע (II)* (pl.) curtain [qeʾ/laʿʾ]

W. Words Occurring 15 Times (48)

אַמְתַּחַת sack; load? ['am/ta/ḥat]

אָרֵךְ; אֶרֶךְ (abs.; const.) slow, long ['ā/rēʾk; 'eʾ/rek]

גָּזַז shear (sheep), cut (hair) [gā/zaʾz]

גֻּלָּה basin [gul/lá']

גָּלוּת exile, deportation; exiles [gā/lûʾt]

גָּלַל (I) roll [gā/laʾl]

גְּעָרָה (n.) rebuke; threat [gəʿ/ā/rá']

גָּרָה* (Pi) go to law [gā/rá'ʾ]

קַשׁ stubble [qaš]

רְבָבָה very great multitude; ten thousand [rəbā/bá']

רַב(-)שָׁקֵה (Assyrian office?) cup-bearer [rab(-/)šā/qēʾh]

רָגַם (v.) stone (someone) [rā/gaʾm]

רֵיקָם (adv.) emptily [rê/qāʾm]

רַךְ (adj.) tender, frail [rak]

שְׂחוֹק laughter [śəḥôq]

שֶׂכֶל, שֵׂכֶל insight, understanding [śeʾ/kel, śēʾ/kel]

שַׂלְמָה (I) mantle, wrapper (cf. שִׂמְלָה, 5.J) [śal/má']

שָׁוָה (I) be(come) like, equal [šā/wá']

שֶׁפֶט* (pl.) judgment; (ext.) punishment [šeʾ/peṭʾ]

דֶּשֶׁן fat; fatty ashes [deʾ/šen]

הָלַל (III) be deluded [hā/laʾl]

חָצָה divide [ḥā/ṣá']

יֹשֶׁר straightness, uprightness [yōʾ/šer]

כָּבַשׁ subdue, subject [kā/baʾš]

כָּלִיל (adj.) entire, whole; (n.) entirety [kā/líʾl]

מֹאזְנַיִם (d.) scales, balance [mō/zəná/yim]

מִבְטָח trust, confidence [mib/ṭāʾḥ]

מוּר* (Ni, intrans.) change; (Hi) exchange [mûr*]

(I) מְחִיר equivalent value, market price [məḥîr]

מִלֻּאִים consecration, ordination [mil/luʾ/ʾîm]

מִקְנֶה acquisition [miq/nâ']

נָגַן (Qal ptc.) musician, string-player; (Pi) play a stringed instrument [nā/ḡán]

סַל basket [sal]

(II) עָצַב find fault with, hurt ['ā/ṣab]

עֵקֶב (to the) end; reward; (conj.) because (of) ['ē'/qeb]

עֲרָפֶל darkness, gloom ['ărā/pé'l]

עָרַץ be afraid, alarmed ['ā/ráṣ]

עָשׂוֹר (group of) ten ['ā/śô'r]

עֹשֶׁק oppression ['ō'/šeq]

פּוּחַ (v.) blow, blad [pú'aḥ]

פָּצָה open up [pā/ṣâ']

צִיץ; צִיצָה (s. m.; f.) blossom (I); (artificial) flower (II) [ṣîṣ; ṣi/ṣâ']

(I) צֶלֶם image [ṣe'/lem]

צֶמֶד yoke, team; (ext.) acre [ṣe'/med]

צָמַת (v.) silence; (Ni) be silenced [ṣā/mát]

קָדַד bow down, kneel down [qā/dád]

(II) קָצַר be (too) short [qā/ṣár]

רָוָה drink one's fill [rā/wá']

רֹמַח* (pl.) lances [rō'/maḥ*]

רְמִיָּה slackness (I?); deceit (II?) [rəmiy/yá']

(I) שִׁבֹּלֶת ear (of grain), bunch of twigs [šib/bō'/let]

(I) שׁוּר* gaze on, regard [šûr*]

שָׁעָה look, gaze [šā/'â']

שֶׁרֶץ (coll.) swarming things, swarm [še'/reṣ]

תֹּאַר form, shape [tō'/ʾar]

תָּם (adj.) complete, right, peaceful [tām]

תַּנּוּר oven, furnace [tan/nú'r]

תַּנִּין; תַּנִּים sea monster [tan/nî'n; tan/nî'm]

תְּרָפִים idols, household gods [tərā/p̄î'm]

X. Words Occurring 14 Times (68)

אֵזוֹר waistcloth, loincloth ['ē/zô'r]

(I) אֵיתָן (adj., n.) perennial; (met.) constant ['ê/tā'n]

אָנַף be angry ['ā/náp̄]

בּוּז show contempt for, despise [bûz]

(III) בַּר grain [bar]

בְּרִיא fat [bā/rîʾ]

גְּאֻלָּה right (duty) of redemption [gəʾul/lấ]

גָּבִיעַ (drinking) bowl, cup [gā/bîʿaʿ]

גָּעַר (v.) reproach [gā/ʿár]

דֶּגֶל banner [deʹgel]

דַּק (adj.) scanty, fine [daq]

דֶּשֶׁא grass [deʹšeʾ]

הָמַם (I) confuse, disturb [hā/mám]

זוּ (dem. and rel. pron.; c.) this [zû]

חוֹתָם (I) (n.) seal [ḥô/tā́m]

חָכָה await [ḥā/kấ]

חַלָּה (ring-shaped) bread [ḥal/lấ]

טוּל* (Hi) throw [ṭûlʹ]

יַבָּשָׁה dry land [yab/bā/šấ]

יָגוֹן torment, grief [yā/ḡôʹn]

יְרֻשָּׁה property [yəruš/šấ]

כָּבֵד (II) liver; (liver-) divination [kā/bḗd]

כְּהֻנָּה priesthood [kəhun/nấ]

כָּרָה (I) excavate, dig [kā/rấ]

כַּרְמֶל (I) orchard [kar/melʹ]

לָוָה (II) borrow; (Hi) lend to [lā/wấ]

לַפִּיד torch; (ext.) lightning [lap/pîʹd]

מָחַץ dash, beat to pieces [mā/ḥáṣ]

מִכְשׁוֹל offense, obstacle [mik/šôʹl]

מָן (I) manna [mān]

מַעֲרָב (II) sunset, west [ma!/ʿărā́b]

מְצִלָּה; מְצִלְתַּיִם* (pl.) bell; (d.) cymbals [məṣil/lấ*; məṣil/ta/yim]

מָרַט pluck (hair) [mā/raʹṭ]

מַשְׂכִּיל (type of) psalm [maś/kîʹl]

נְגִינָה string music [nəḡî/nấ]

נֶתֶק a skin disease [ne'/teq]

סָתַם plug up, stop up [sā/taʹm]

עֶגְלָה (I) heifer [ʿeḡ/lấ]

עֲדִי (s. and coll.) ornament(s) [ʿădî]

עָכַר (make) trouble; make (someone) taboo? [ʿā/kaʹr]

עָצֵל (adj.) slow, sluggish [ʿā/ṣḗl]

עָקֵב heel [ʿā/qḗb]

עָרָה* (Ni) be poured out; (Pi) empty out [ʿā/rấ*]

פָּגַשׁ meet [pā/ḡaʹš]

פִּסֵּחַ (adj.) lame [pis/sḗaḥ]

פְּעֻלָּה work, deeds; reward, wages [pəʿul/lấ]

פֶּרֶד mule [peʹ/red]

פָּרַס break [pā/raʹs]

פַּת bit, morsel [pat]

צָבָא go to war, serve [ṣā/bāʾ]

צְבִי (II) gazelle (species) [ṣəbî]

צַיִד (I) game; hunting [ṣa/yid]

צַעַד walking; (pl.) steps [ṣa/ʿad]

קְבוּרָה burial, grave [qəbû/rá']

קֶמַח flour [qe/maḥ]

קָצַץ cut off, trim [qā/ṣáṣ]

קֶשֶׁר conspiracy [qe/šer]

רָוַח feel relieved; (Hi) smell, enjoy the smell of [rā/waḥ]

רֵיק, רֵק (adj.) empty [rêq, rēq]

רָעֵב (stat.) be hungry [rā/ʿḗb]

(II) שִׂיחַ (object of) concern, interest [śí'aḥ]

שְׁאֵלָה request [šə'ē/lá']

שָׁאַף gasp, pant (for) [šā/'áp̄]

שָׁרַץ swarm, teem [šā/ráṣ]

(II) תּוֹר turtledove [tôr]

תּוֹשָׁב sojourner, alien [tô/šā'b]

(I) תַּחַשׁ porpoise? dolphin? [ta/ḥaš]

תַּן* (pl.) jackal [tanⁿ]

Y. Words Occurring 13 Times (63)

אָנָּא (imprec.) please! I pray! [ʾān/nā'']

אָרַג weave; (Qal ptc.) weaver [ʾā/ra/ḡ]

בָּחִיר (adj.) chosen, elect [bā/ḥír]

(II) בַּת bath (liquid measure) [bat]

גֹּדֶל greatness [gō/del]

גָּדֵר (stone) wall [gā/dḗr]

גְּוִיָּה body [gəwiy/yá']

דָּקַק crush [dā/qáq]

(II) הַוָּה (n.) ruin [haw/wá']

הָלְאָה (adv.) out there, onward [hā/lə'á']

וָו* (pl.) nail [wāwⁿ]

זֵד (adj.) arrogant [zēd]

זוֹב (mucous or blood) discharge [zób]

זָמַם think, plan [zā/mám]

זְנוּנִים prostitution [zənû/ní'm]

חָבַק embrace [ḥā/báq]

חָזֶה chest (of animal) [ḥā/ze'h]

חַנּוּן (adj.) gracious, friendly [ḥan/nú'n]

חָנֵף (adj.) godless [ḥā/nḗp̄]

(I) חֹר* (pl.) noble [ḥōrⁿ]

טָהֳרָה (cultic) purity [ṭo/ḥŏrá']

טִיט wet clay, mud [ṭîṭ]

טַעַם (n.) taste [ṭa/ʿam]

יְבוּל (n.) produce [yəbûl]

יָלִיד son; one born a slave [yā/lí'd]

יְשִׁימוֹן desert, wilderness [yəši/mô'n]

(IV) כֹּפֶר bribe [kō/p̄er]

לוּלֵא; לוּלֵי (conj.) if not [lû/lē''; lû/lē']

לְלָאֹת loops [lu!/lā/ʾō′t]

מַבּוּל flood [mab/bú′l]

מוֹסָד foundation (-wall), base [mô/sā′d]

מַחְמָד (something) desirable [mah̠/mā′d]

מַחְסוֹר (n.) want, need [mah̠/sô′r]

מָנָה portion, part, share [mā/nâ′]

מַעְגָּל (II) track, rut [maʿ/gā′l]

מֵצַח forehead [mē′/ṣah̠]

מִרְעֶה pasture [mir/ʿe′h]

מַרְפֵּא (I) healing [mar/pē′ʾ]

נְבָלָה stupidity [nəbā/lâ′]

נָעִים (adj.) pleasant, lovely [nā/ʿî′m]

עָטַף (II) grow weak, faint [ʿā/ṭa′p̄]

פָּאַר* (II) (Pi) glorify [pā/ʾa′r]

פֶּלֶא (n.) marvel [peʾ/leʾ]

פְּנִימָה (adv.) into, inside [pəni/mâ′]

פָּקִיד officer [pā/qi′d]

צָחַק laugh; (Pi) joke, play [ṣā/h̠a′q]

צְפַרְדֵּעַ (coll.) frogs [ṣəp̄ar/dē′aʿ]

קָבַב curse [qā/ba′b]

קָבַל* (Pi) accept, receive [qā/ba′l]

קָו; קַו (I) (measuring-) cord [qāw; qaw]

קַל (adj.) light, quick [qal]

קֵן nest; (pl.) compartments [qēn]

רָגַע (intrans.) crust over, come to rest [rā/ḡa′ʿ]

רַחוּם (adj.) compassionate [ra!/h̠ú′m]

שְׂרֵפָה (place of) burning, conflagration [śərē/p̄ā′]

שׁוֹאָה (trad.) ruin, storm; (better) pit [šô/ʾā′]

שׁוּט* (I) roam about, rove [šûṭ]

שְׁחִין boil, ulcer [šəh̠în]

שָׁחַר (II) be intent on; (Pi) seek [šā/h̠a′r]

שִׁכּוֹר (adj.) drunk(en) [šik/kô′r]

שָׁלַל (v.) plunder, spoil [šā/la′l]

תָּא guardroom [tā′ʾ]

תַּעַר razor, knife [ta′/ʿar]

Z. Words Occurring 12 Times (78)

אַדֶּרֶת splendor; robe [ʾad/de′/ret]

אַיִן (II) (interr.) (from) where? [ʾa′/yin]

אָנַח* (Ni) sigh, groan [ʾā/na′h̠]

אֹפֶה baker [ʾō/p̄e′h]

בַּהֶרֶת white patch of skin [ba!/he′/ret]

בּוּז (I) contempt [bú′z]

בּוּס* trample down [bús]

בִּי (formula to open conversation with superiors; lit "on me") [bî]

גַּב (I) something arched; torus, boss [gab]

גְּדוּלָה (?) greatness [gǝdûl/lấ]

גּוּר* (III) be afraid (of) [gûr"]

גָּזַר (I) cut; decide [gā/zaŕ]

גֻּלְגֹּלֶת skull [gul/gō'/let]

דֹּב (n.; c.) bear [dōb]

זָעַם (v.) curse, scold [zā/ʿaḿ]

חָבֵר (m.) companion [ḥā/bēŕ]

חַיָּה (II) life; greed, appetite [ḥay/yấ]

חֲלִיפָה change, relief [ḥăli/p̄ấ]

חָלָק (adj.) smooth [ḥā/lā'q]

חֹמֶר (III) *homer* (dry measure) [ḥō'/mer]

חָפָה (v.) cover, veil [ḥā/p̄ấ]

חָפֵץ having pleasure in; willing [ḥā/p̄ē'ṣ]

חֵקֶר searching [ḥē'/qer]

חֹשֵׁב weaver, technician [ḥō/šē'b]

טֶבַח (I) slaughtering [ṭe'/baḥ]

טוּחַ* (v.) plaster, overlay [ṭûaḥ"]

יוֹנֵק suckling; infant [yô/nē'q]

יָחִיד (adj.) only [yā/ḥî'd]

יֶרַח (I) (lunar) month [yǝ'/raḥ]

כַּמָּה, כַּמֶּה (interr. pron.) how much? how many? [kam/mấ, kam/me'h]

כַּר (I) ram; battering ran [kar]

לְבֵנָה brick; paving-stone [lǝbē/nấ]

לַהַב flame [la'/hab]

לָוָה (I) accompany; (Ni) be joined, join [lā/wấ]

לַחַץ oppression, affliction [la'/ḥaṣ]

מִבְחָר (I) (the) choicest, best [mib/ḥāŕ]

מֶגֶד yield of fruit; (f. pl.) precious gifts [me'/ḡed]

מַד clothing, garment [mad]

מְהוּמָה confusion, panic [mǝhû/mấ]

מוֹטָה yoke, collar; carrying poles? [mô/ṭấ]

מוֹסֵר fetter(s), chain(s) [mô/sēŕ]

מוֹרָא fear, terror [mô/rā']

מַסַּע breaking (camp), departure [mas/saʿ]

מְצוֹלָה deep, depths [mǝṣô/lấ]

מִצְנֶפֶת headband, turban [miṣ/ne'/p̄et]

מִקְצוֹעַ corner [miq/ṣô'aʿ]

מֹר myrrh [mōr]

מַרְאָה vision [mar/ʾấ]

מְשׁוּבָה* defection [mǝšû/bấ"]

מָתוֹק sweet [mā/tô'q]

נָזַר dedicate oneself (to a deity) [nā/zaŕ]

נָפַח (v.) blow [nā/p̄aḥ]

נְצִיב (I) pillar; garrison [nəṣîb]

נָשַׁךְ (I) bite [nā/šaḵ]

נֶשֶׁךְ interest (on debt) [neʿ/šek]

נֶשֶׁף twilight, darkness [neʿ/šep̄]

נֵתַח piece (of meat) [nēʿ/taḥ]

סָעַד support, sustain [sā/ʿad]

עָוַת (?) pervert; (Pi) make crooked, falsify (I עוּת?) [ʿā/waṯ]

עָמִית fellow, comrade [ʿā/mîṯ]

עָקָר (adj.) barren [ʿā/qāʾr]

עֹרֵב (I) raven [ʿō/rēʾb]

פֶּטֶר; פִּטְרָה firstborn [peʿ/ṭer; piṭ/rāʾ]

צֶמַח (coll.) growth, what sprouts [ṣeʿ/maḥ]

קָדְקֹד crown of head [qod/qōʾd]

קוֹץ thorn bush [qôṣ]

קָצִין leader [qā/ṣîʾn]

רֹאֶה seer; (seeing) visions [rō/ʾeʾh]

רֹאשׁ (II) poisonous plant; (ext.) poison [rōʾš]

רָבַע (II) (den.; Qal ptc. pass.) squared [rā/baʿʿ]

רַגְלִי foot soldier [raḡ/lîʾ]

רִיק (n.) emptiness; (adj.) empty, worthless [rîq]

רִקְמָה fabric (of varied colors) [riq/māʾ]

שָׁסָה (v.) plunder; (Qal ptc.) plunderer [šā/sāʾ]

שָׁרַק (v.) whistle [šā/raʾq]

תּוּשִׁיָּה success [tû/šiy/yāʾ]

תִּיכוֹן (adj.) the middle [tî/kôʾn]

תָּמָר (I) date palm [tā/māʾr]

AA. Words Occurring 11 Times (64)

אֲבָל (interj.) truly; (advs. con.) but, however [ʾăḇāl]

אֲנָחָה (n.) sigh, groan [ʾănā/ḥāʾ]

אִסָּר vow of abstinence [ʾis/sāʾr]

אָרַשׂ* (Pi, Pu) become engaged [ʾā/raʾś]

אֶתְנַן gift [ʾeṯ/naʾn]

בָּדָד solitude; (adv.) alone [bā/dāʾd]

גָּאַל* (II) (Ni) become polluted [gā/ʾalʾ]

גָּזִית hewn stone, ashlar [gā/zîʾṯ]

גֵּרָה (I) cud [gē/rāʾ]

דָּקַר pierce [dā/qaʾr]

דָּשֵׁן (stat.) become fat [dā/šēʾn]

הָדַף shove [hā/daʾp̄]

הֲלֹם (adv.) (to) here [hălōm]

זָדוֹן arrogance [zā/dôʾn]

זַךְ (adj.) pure [zak]

זָנָב tail; (met.) end [zā/nāʾb]

(I) חֹוחַ thorn bush, thorn [ḥô'aḥ]

חָמֹות mother-in-law [ḥā/mố't]

חָמֵץ something leavened [ḥā/mḗṣ]

(I) חָנֵף be godless, defiled [ḥā/nấp̄]

חַרְטֹם soothsayer-priest [ḥar/ṭố'm]

חָשַׁק (v.) love [ḥā/šá'q]

טָבַח (v.) slaughter [ṭā/ba'ḥ]

טָעַם taste, eat [ṭā/'á'm]

יִדְּעֹנִי spirit of the dead; soothsayer [yid/də'ō/nî']

יָקַץ (intrans.) awake, wake up [yā/qá'ṣ]

יָקַר be difficult; be valued; be precious, rare [yā/qá'r]

יֹתֶרֶת (extra) lobes of (animal) liver; (met.) what is redundant [yố/te'/ret]

כָּנַס gather, collect [kā/ná's]

לָבִיא (poet.) lioness [lā/bî']

לָהַט consume, burn (I?); (Pi) devour (II?) [lā/ha'ṭ]

(II) מָגֹור* (pl.) sojourning; alien citizenship [mā/ḡố'r*]

מְחִתָּה terror [məḥit/tấ]

מְצָד stronghold [məṣād]

(I) נֵבֶל (storage-) jar [nḗ'/bel]

נָבַע (v.) bubble (brook) [nā/ba'']

(II) נָעַר shake [nā/'á'r]

סֹלֲלָה siege mound, rampart [sō/lălâ]

סַפִּיר lapis lazuli [sap/pî'r]

עֹולֵל child ['ô/lḗ'l]

עָזַז be strong, prevail ['ā/za'z]

עָמָל labor, exert oneself ['ā/ma'l]

עָנַן* (Pi) cause to appear, conjure up ['ā/na'n*]

עֲצָרָה; עֲצֶרֶת festive assembly ['ăṣā/rấ; 'ăṣe'/ret]

(I) עִקֵּשׁ (adj.) perverted ['iq/qḗ'š]

עָרוּם (adj.) subtle, crafy ['ā/rû'm]

פִּתּוּחַ engravving [pit/tú'aḥ]

פָּתִיל thread, cord [pā/tî'l]

צֶאֱצָא* (pl.) offspring [ṣe!/'ĕṣấ'*]

(I) צוּק* (Hi) press hard, oppress [ṣû̂q*]

(I) קָדֵשׁ (adj.) consecrated; (n.) cult prostitute [qā/dḗ'š]

קֶסֶם divination [qe'/sem]

קָרֵב (adj.) approaching [qā/rḗ'b]

קָרְחָה baldness [qor/ḥấ']

רִבֹּו; רְבֹוא countless; ten thousand [rib/bô'; rib/bô']

(I) רָעַם (v.) storm, thunder [rā/'a'm]

רָקַע stamp; (Pi.) hammer out [rā/qaʻ]

שַׁאֲנָן (adj.) at ease, tranquil [šaʾ!/ʾănāʾn]

שַׁבָּתוֹן sabbath feast [šab/bā/tôʾn]

(I) שֹׁהַם onyx? carnelian? lapis lazuli? [šō/haʾm]

שׁוּל* (pl.) flowing skirt; hem of skirt [šúlˀ]

שַׁוְעָה cry for help [šaw/ʻâʾ]

שֶׁקֶץ (cultic) abomination [še/qeṣ]

שָׁתַל plant, transplant [šā/taʾl]

BB. Words Occurring 10 Times (67)

אִגֶּרֶת (official, commercial) letter [ʾig/geʾ/ret]

אֹדוֹת (prep.) on account of; (conj.) because [ʾō/dōʾt]

אָדַם be red; (Pu ptc.) dyed red [ʾā/daʾm]

אוּץ* urge, be in a hurry; (Hi) urge [ʾúṣˀ]

אֵזוֹב hyssop? [ʾē/zôʾb]

(VI) אֵל (dem. pron.) these [ʾēl]

(I) אֵלוֹן terebinth, tall tree [ʾē/lôʾn]

אֲפֵלָה darkness [ʾăpē/lâʾ]

בִּגְלַל on account of, for the sake of [big/laʾl]

בֶּדֶק chink; leak (in ship) [be/deq]

בִּזָּה plunder (act and objects of) [biz/zâʾ]

בְּכֹרָה rights of firstborn [bəkō/râʾ]

בַּלָּהָה sudden terror [bal/lā/hâʾ]

בְּמוֹ (prep.) in, by [bəmô]

בְּתוּלִים virginity; evidence of virginity [bətû/līʾm]

גְּבוּלָה boundary, territory [gəbú/lâʾ]

גָּדַר erect a wall [gā/daʾr]

(II) גָּלַל Cf. בִּגְלַל

גָּעַל abhor [gā/ʻaʾl]

גָּעַשׁ shake [gā/ʻaʾš]

הַלָּז; הַלָּזֶה (dem. pron., m. and f.; m.) this [hal/lāʾz; hal/lā/zeʾh]

הֶרֶג; הֲרֵגָה (s. m.; f.) killing, murder; slaughter [he/reḡ; hărē/ḡâʾ]

זִיד* treat insolently [zîdˀ]

זֵר molding [zēr]

(II) חָבַל treat badly [ḥā/baʾl]

חָדַשׁ* (Pi) make new, restore [ḥā/daʾšˀ]

חֲלָצַיִם (d.) loins [ḥālā/ṣaʾ/yim]

חֶמְאָה curdled milk [ḥem/ʾâʾ]

חָרֵב (adj.) dry, waste [ḥā/rēʾb]

חָרַץ (I) (idiom.) threaten; settle, determine [ḥā/raṣ]

טָבַע sink in [ṭā/baʿ]

יִתְרוֹן outcome, profit [yit/rốn]

כַּבִּיר strong, powerful [kab/bîr]

כֶּלֶא confinement; prison [keʾ/leʾ]

מִלּוֹא terrace? (construction) fill? [mil/lôʾ]

מִמְכָּר selling, sale [mim/kār]

מִסְתָּר hiding place [mis/tār]

מַצָּב post (of duty) [maṣ/ṣāb]

מָקַק* (Ni) rot [mā/qaq̈]

מִקְרֶה happening, occurrence [miq/reh]

מְרַאֲשׁוֹת head place [məra!/ʾăšốṭ]

מַרְעִית pasturage [mar/ʿîṭ]

נָגַח (v.) gore [nā/g̊aḥ]

נָגַר* (Ni) flow, gush forth [nā/g̊ar̈]

נָהַל* (Pi) lead, guide [nā/hal̈]

נְחוּשָׁה copper, bronze [nəḥû/šấ]

נֶשֶׁק; נֵשֶׁק armor, weaponry [nē/šeq, ne/šeq]

עֵירֹם (adj.) naked; (n.) nakedness [ʿê/rốm]

עָנַג* (Pu ptc.) pampered, spoiled; (Hith) pamper oneself [ʿā/nag̈]

עַפְעַפַּיִם (d.) eyelids?; rays; flashing glance of the eye [ʿap̄/ʿap/pa/yim]

עֲרֵמָה heap [ʿărē/mấ]

עֶרֶשׂ bedstead, couch [ʿe/reś]

פָּזַר (Qal ptc. pass.) dispersed; (Pi) disperse, scatter [pā/zar]

פַּחַת pit [pa/ḥat]

פֶּלֶג (I) canal [pe/leg̈]

פֶּרֶא wild ass, onager? zebra? [pe/reʾ]

פָּרַק tear away [pā/raq]

צָמֵא (stat.) be thirsty [ṣā/mēʾ]

קַדְמֹנִי (I) (adj.) eastern [qad/mō/nî]

קָמָה standing grain [qā/mấ]

קֶרֶס* (pl.) hook [qe/res̈]

שָׂבֵעַ (adj.) full, satisfied [śā/bḗaʿ]

שָׁמֵן (adj.) fat [šā/mḗn]

שְׁפִי (I) barrenness, baldness [šəp̄î]

שְׁרִרוּת hardness, stubbornness [šəri/rúṭ]

תַּהְפּוּכָה* (pl.) perversity [tah/pû/kấ̈]

תְּמוּנָה form, image [təmû/nấ]

SECTION 6: ARAMAIC VOCABULARY (648)

A. Words Occurring More Than 50 Times (15)

אֱדַיִן (adv.) then [ʾĕda/yin] 57

אֱלָהּ §god; God [ʾĕlāh] 95

אֲמַר ‡say; command [ʾămar] 73

בְּ †(pref. prep.) in, through, by (means of), for 50

דִּי; דְּ (rel. part.) what, that which [dî] 292

הֲוָה §be, happen, exist [hăwâ] 70

וְ †(pref. conj.) and, also, even 50

כְּ †(pref. prep.) like, as 70

כֹּל †all, whole [kōl] 82

לְ †(pref. prep.) for, to 70

לָא; לָהּ ‡(adv.) not [lāʾ; lâ] 70

מֶלֶךְ †king [me/lek] 178

מַלְכוּ §kingship; kingdom [mal/kú] 57

מִן †(prep.) from, out of [min] 100

עַל †(prep.) on, upon; against; toward; concerning [ʿal] 98

B. Words Occurring 50 through 20 Times (27)

אֱנָשׁ (s. def. coll.) mankind [ʾĕnāš] 25

אֲרַע (the) earth; (ext.) inferior [ʾăraʿ] 21

בַּיִת †house; (ext.) temple [ba/yit] 44

בְּנָה ‡build [bənâ] 22

גְּבַר ‡man [gəbar] 21

דְּהַב gold [dəhab] 23

דְּנָה (dem. pron. m.; adj.) this [dənâ] 42

חֲזָה ‡see, perceive [ḥăzâ] 31

חֵיוָה beast, animal [ḥê/wâ] 20

חֵלֶם §dream [ḥē/lem] 22

טְעֵם ‡understanding, good sense; report [ṭəʿēm] 30

יְדַע ‡know [yəda] 47

יְהַב ‡give [yəhab] 28

מִלָּה †word [mil/lâ] 24

עֲבַד ‡do, make [ʿăbad] 28

עַד †(prep.) up to, until; (conj.) until [ʿad] 34

עִם †(prep.) with [ʿim] 22

עֲנָה‡ answer; (ext.) begin to speak [ʹănâ] 30

פַּרְזֶל§ iron [par/zeʹl] 20

פְּשַׁר‡ interpretation [pəšar] 31

קֳבֵל (prep.) before, in front of [qŏbēl] 29

קֳדָם‡ (prep.) before, in front of [qŏdām] 42

קוּם‡* stand (rise) up [qûm*]

רַב† (adj.) great; chief [rab] 23

שִׂים†* set, lay, put [śîm*] 26

שְׁמַיִן§ heaven, sky [šəmaʹ/yin] 38

שְׁנָה‡ be different, diverse [šənâ] 21

C. Words Occurring 19 through 13 Times (34)

אִיתַי existence; there is (are) [ʹi/taʹi] 17

אִלֵּך (dem. pron.) these [ʹil/lēʹk] 14

אֲנָה§ (pers. pron.) I [ʹănâ] 16

אַנְתָּה (pers. pron., m. s.) you [ʹan/tâʹ] 15

אֲתָה‡ come [ʹătâ] 16

גַּו, גוֹ‡ interior [gaw, gô] 13

דֵּך, דָּך (dem. adj., s. m.; f.) that [dēk, dāk] 13

דָת† decree; state law, law [dāt] 14

הוּא† (pers. pron.) he; (dem. adj.) that [hûʹ] 14

הֵיכַל‡ palace; temple [hê/kaʹl] 13

הֵן† (conj.) if; whether [hēn] 15

חַד one [ḥad] 14

חֲוָה‡* (Pa, Ha) make known [ḥăwâ*] 15

חַכִּים§ (adj.) wise (man) [ḥak/kîʹm] 14

יַד‡ hand; (ext.) power [yad] 17

יוֹם† day [yôm] 15

כְּסַף‡ silver [kəsap] 13

כְּעַן now [kəʻan] 13

מָה†; מָא (interr. pron.) what?; (rel. pron.) what, that which [mâ; māʹ] 14

נְהַר‡ stream, river [nəhar] 15

נוּר fire [nûr] 17

עֲבַר‡ the opposite bank (i.e., west of the Euphrates) [ʻăbar] 14

עֲלַל† go in [ʻălal] 14

עָלַם§ remote time, eternity [ʻā/laʹm] 19

עַם† (coll.) people [ʻam] 15

צְלֵם‡ statue [ṣəlēm] 17

קַדִּישׁ§ (adj.) holy [qad/dîʹš] 13

קֶרֶן† horn [qeʹ/ren] 14

רֵאשׁ‡ head; beginning [rēʹš] 14

שַׂגִּיא‡ (adj.) great; much, many; (adv.) very [śag/gîʾ] 13

שְׁכַח*‡ (Ha) find [šəkaḥ*] 18

שְׁלַח‡ send [šəlaḥ] 14

שָׁלְטָן lordship, dominion [šol/ṭāʾn] 14

תְּלָת; תְּלָתִין (m.) three; (pl.) thirty [təlāt; təlā/tîʾn] 13

D. Words Occurring 12 through 10 Times (29)

אָחֳרָן; אָחֳרִי (s. m.; f.) another [ʾā/ḥŏrāʾn; ʾā/ḥŏrîʾ] 11

אַרְיֵה† lion [ʾar/yēʾh] 10

אַתּוּן furnace [ʾat/tûʾn] 10

בְּהַל*‡ (Pa) frighten; (Hithpe) hurry [bəhal*] 11

בֵּן*† (pl.) son (cf. II בַּר, 6.E) [bēn*] 11

בְּעָה‡ seek, request [bəʿâ] 12

גֹּב‡ pit [gōb] 10

דְּקַק‡ break into pieces [dəqaq] 10

הִמּוֹ§; הִמּוֹן (pers. pron. m.) they, them [him/môʾ; him/môʾn] 12

זְמָן† time [zəmān] 11

חֵזוּ vision; appearance [ḥēzû] 12

יְכֵל‡ (stat.) be able; overpower [yəkil] 12

כְּתָב† writing, inscription; document; rule [kətāb] 12

מְדִינָה province [mədî/nāʾ] 11

מַן‡ (interr. pron.) who? (rel. pron.) whoever [man] 10

נְפַל‡ fall (down) [nəpal] 11

נְפַק go out [nəpaq] 11

סְגִד‡ pay homage (to) [səgid] 12

עִדָּן time [ʿid/dāʾn] 12

עִלָּי superior, highest; (ext.) most high God [ʿil/lāʾi] 10

פֶּחָה† governor [pe!/ḥāʾ] 10

פְּלַח‡ serve (God) [pəlaḥ] 10

צְבָה long to, desire to [ṣəbâ] 10

קְרָא‡ shout; read [qərāʾ] 11

רוּחַ† wind; spirit [rûʾaḥ] 11

רְמָה‡ throw; place; impose [rəmâ] 12

שְׁאָר† remainder, rest [šə ʾār] 12

שַׁלִּיט† (adj.) mighty, powerful [šal/lîʾṭ] 10

שֵׁם‡ name [šum] 12

E. Words Occurring 9 and 8 Times (29)

אַב‡ father [ʾab] 9

אֶבֶן† stone [ʾe/ben] 8

אֲחַשְׁדַּרְפַּן*	(pl.) satrap [ʾăḥaš/dar/paʹn*] 9	כַּשְׂדָּי	Chaldean(s); (ext.) astrologers [kaś/dāʹi] 9
אֻמָּה†‡	nation(s) [ʾum/mâʹ] 8	כְּתַב‡	write [kətab] 8
אַרְבַּע*†	(f.) four [ʾar/baʻ*] 8	לֵב; לְבַב‡	heart [lēb; ləbab] 8
אֲתַר; בַּ(אֲ)תַר	trace, place; (prep.) in place (of), after [ʾătar; bā(ʾ)/taʹr] 8	מְטָא	extend, reach [məṭāʾ] 8
בַּר† (I)	field [bar] 8	נְחָשׁ§	copper, bronze [nəḥāš] 9
בַּר† (II)	son (cf. בֵּן, 6.D) [bar] 8	סְלִק‡	go (come) up [səliq] 8
גְּלָה‡†	reveal; (Ha) deport [gəlâ] 9	עֲדָה‡	go (away) [ʿădâ] 9
חָכְמָה†‡	wisdom [ḥok/mâʹ] 8	קְרֵב‡	approach, step up to [qərēb] 9
חֲסַף	(formed) clay [ḥăsap̄] 9	קִרְיָה†‡	town, city [qir/yāʹ] 9
יְקַד	burn [yəqad] 8	רַבְרְבָן*	(pl.) lord, noble [rab/rəbʹān*] 8
יַתִּיר	(adj.) extraordinary; (adv.) extremely [yat/tîr] 8	רָז	secret [rāz] 9
כָּהֵן‡	priest [kā/hēʹn] 8	שֵׁיזִב	(loanword) rescue, save [šê/ziʹb] 9
כֵּן†‡	(adv.) thus, so [kēn] 8	שְׁמַע‡	hear; (Hithpa) obey [šəmaʻ] 9
		תּוּב*	return [tûb*] 8

F. Words Occurring 7 Times (27)

אֲבַד‡	go to ruin, perish [ʾăbad]	חַיִל†	strength; army [ḥaʹyil]
אֲזַל‡	go (away) [ʾăzal]	יְקָר	honor, majesty [yəqār]
אֲכַל‡	eat [ʾăkal]	כְּלַל*‡	(Sha) finish [kəlal]
אָסְפַּרְנָא	(adv.) exactly, eagerly [ʾos/parʹnāʾ]	כְּנָת*†	(pl.) colleague [kənāt*]
אֱסָר‡	interdict [ʾĕsār]	לָהֵן (II)	(conj.) unless, except; (advs.) but, but rather [lā/hēʹn]
דּוּר*†	live, dwell [dûr*]	לִשָּׁן§	tongue; (ext.) language [liš/šāʹn]
הִיא†	(pers. pron.) she [hîʾ]	מְאָה‡	hundred [məʾâ]
הֲלַךְ‡†	go [hălak]	מָאן*	(pl.) vessel [māʾn*]
חַי†	(adj.) living, alive; (pl.) life [ḥai]	נְתַן‡	give [nətan]

עֶבֶד servant [ʿăbēd]

עֲשַׂר‡; עֶשְׂרִין (m.) ten; (pl.) twenty [ʿăśar; ʿeś/rî′n]

קְטַל‡ kill [qəṭal]

קָל§ voice; sound [qāl]

רְגַל*‡ (d.) foot [rəḡal"]

רְשַׁם‡ write [rəšam]

שְׁלֵט‡ rule; overpower [šəlēṭ]

שְׁנָה‡ (I) year [šənâ]

תּוֹר* (pl.) bull, ox, steer [tôr"]

G. Words Occurring 6 Times (22)

אִילָן tree [ʾi/lā′n]

אָשַׁף‡ conjurer [ʾā/ša′p]

בְּטֵל‡ (intrans.) stop; be discontinued [baṭēl]

גְּזַר‡ (ptc. pl.) astrologers; (Hith) be cut out [gəzar]

דְּחַל* (ptc.) fear, frightening [dəḥal"]

הֲ־† (pref. interr. part.)

זִיו brightness [zîw]

חֲבַל*‡ (Pa) hurt, injure [ḥăbal"]

חֲיָה‡ (v.) live [ḥăyâ]

חֲמַר‡ wine [ḥămar]

מִשְׁכַּב‡ bed, couch [miš/ka′b]

נְחַת‡ come down [nəḥat]

סָפַר§ clerk, secretary [sā/pā′r]

עֲבִידָה work; administration [ʿăbî/dā′]

פֻּם mouth; (ext.) entrance [pum]

פִּתְגָם†‡ word; decree [pit/ḡā′m]

רְבָה‡ become great, grow up [rəbâ]

רְבִיעָי‡ fourth [rəbî/ʿā′i]

רַעְיוֹן* (pl.) thought [raʿ/yô′n"]

שְׁאֵל‡ ask, desire, require [šə′ēl]

שְׁבַע‡ seven [šəbaʿ]

שְׁרָה‡ loosen [šərâ]

H. Words Occurring 5 Times (35)

אֲלוּ (interj.) behold! [ʾălú]

אִלֵּין (dem. pron.) these [ʾil/lê′n]

אָע wood [ʾāʿ]

אֲרוּ (interj.) behold! [ʾărú]

בְּקַר*‡ (Pa) search [bəqar"]

בְּרַם (advs. adv.) but, yet, only [baram]

גְּשֵׁם body [gəšēm]

דָּא (dem. pron. f.) this [dāʾ]

דִּין† (n.) right, judgment; council of judges [dîn]

חַרְטֹם‡ magician [ḥar/ṭṓm]

טַל‡ dew [ṭal]

יַצִּיב (adj.) reliable [yaṣ/ṣîb]

יְתִב sit down; dwell [yətib]

כְּנֵמָא (adv.) thus, so [kənē/mā']

לֵילִי§ night [lê/lê']

מְלַל‡* (Pa) speak [məlal"]

מְנָה‡ count, number [mənâ]

סְגַן‡* (pl.) prefect, governor [səḡan"]

סוֹף end [sôp̄]

סְפַר‡ book [səp̄ar]

סָרַךְ* (pl.) official [sā/rak"]

עַיִן‡ eye ['a/yin]

עֲשַׂב‡ grass; (coll.) greens ['ăśab]

צְבַע* (Pa) wet, moisten [ṣəbā'"]

רְבוּ‡ greatness [rəbû]

רוּם‡ height [rûm]

שָׂב* (pl.) elders [śāb"]

שְׁבַח*‡ (Pa) praise [šəbaḥ"]

שְׁבַק leave [šəbaq]

שָׁעָה moment [šā/'ấ']

שֵׁת; שִׁתִּין (m.) six; (pl.) sixty [šēt; šit/tî'n]

שְׁתָה‡ drink [šətâ]

תְּחוֹת§ (prep.) under [təḥôt]

תַּקִּיף‡† (adj.) strong, mighty [taq/qî'p̄"]

תְּקֵף‡ (stat.) be(come) strong [təqip̄]

I. Words Occurring 4 Times (40)

אַל‡† (neg.) not ['al]

אַמָּה*‡† (pl.) cubit ['am/mấ'"]

אִנּוּן (pers. pron.) they ['in/nú'n]

אֲנַחְנָא§ (pers. pron.) we ['ănǎ/ḥənā']

בְּרִךְ‡‡ (II) bless [bərak]

גָּלוּ‡ exile [gā/lú']

הַדָּבַר* (pl.) royal official [had/dā/ba'r]

זְמָר (string-) music [zəmār]

זַן*† (pl.) kind, sort [zan"]

חֲבַר*‡; חַבְרָה (pl. m.; f.) companion [ḥăbar"; ḥab/rấ'"]

חֲלַף‡ pass by (over) [ḥălap̄]

חֲנֻכָּה dedication [ḥănuk/kấ']

טְרַד drive away [ṭərad]

כְּהֵל (stat.) be able [kəhēl]

כְּעֶנֶת (adv.) and now [kə'e/net]

כְּפַת be bound, tied up [kəpat]

מִדָּה tax, tribute [mid/dấ']

מְדוֹר dwelling [mədôr]

מְחָא strike [məḥā']

מַנְדַּע understanding [man/da'']

מָרֵא lord [mā/rē'']

מַשְׁרוֹקִי pipe (musical instrument) [maš/rô/qî']

נְבִיא‡ prophet [nəḇî']

נָדַב*‡ (Hithpa) bestow; be willing; (ptc.) disposed, willing [nəḏaḇ*]

נְזַק§ (ptc.) suffer loss; (Ha ptc., inf.) wrong, injure [nəzaq]

עֶלְיוֹן*‡ (pl.) the Most High ['el/yô'n*]

עֲנַף* (pl.) branch, bough ['ǎnaḇ*]

עֲרַב*‡ (Pa) mix ['ǎraḇ*]

פְּסַנְתֵּרִין harp [pəsan/tē/rî'n]

פַּרְשֶׁגֶן copy [par/še'/ḡen]

צְלַח*‡ (Ha) cause to prosper; make progress [ṣəlaḥ*]

צִפַּר*§ (pl.) bird [ṣip/pa'r*]

קַיתְרֹם (?) kithara (kind of lyre or lute) [qai/tərō's]

רוּם*†‡ raise oneself; (Pol) praise [rûm*]

שַׂבְּכָא lyre? [śab/kā']

שְׁלָה†; שָׁלוּ negligence [(Q) šā/lû'; šā/lú']

שְׁלָם§ well-being, good health, welfare [šəlām]

שְׁפֵל*‡ (Ha) bring low, humble [šəp̄ēl*]

תַּמָּה (adv.) there [tam/mâ']

תְּרֵין; תַּרְתֵּין (s. m.; f.) two [tərên; tar/tê'n]

J. Words Occurring 3 Times (66)

אֵב†; אִנְבָּא (abs.; emph.) fruit ['ēḇ; 'in/bā']

אִגְּרָה§; אִגְּרָא letter (correspondence) ['ig/gərá; 'ig/gərā']

אֲזָה light a fire, heat ['ǎzâ]

אַחַר*†‡ (adv. pl.) after ['a!/ḥa'r]

אֵל*†‡; אֵלֶּה (dem. pl.) these ['ēl*; 'ē'l/leh]

אֲמַן*‡ (Ha) trust in ['ǎma'n*]

אִמַּר*‡ (pl.) (sacrificial) lamb ['im/ma'r*]

אֱסוּר*‡ bond(s), fetter(s); (pl., ext.) imprisonment ['ĕsûr]

אַף*† (conj.) also ['aḇ]

אֶצְבַּע*†‡ finger; toe ['eṣ/ba'ʿ*]

אַרְגְּוָן purple (garment) ['ar/gəwā'n]

אֹשׁ* (pl. def.) foundation ['ōš*]

אָת*§ (pl.) sign ['āt*]

בָּאתַר after [bā'/ta'r]

בְּלוֹ tribute [bəlô]

בְּעֵל‡ owner, master, lord [bə'ēl]

בְּשַׂר‡ flesh [bəśar]

גְּנַז*†‡ (pl.) treasure [gənaz*]

גַּף* (pl.) wing [gaḇ*]

דִּכֵּן (dem. pron. c.) that [dik/kē'n]

דְּכַר* (pl.) ram [dəkar*]

הַדַּר*‡ (Pa) glorify [hădar"]

הֲדַר‡ (n.) splendor, majesty [hădar]

הֲלָךְ toll duty [hălāk]

הַמּוּנְךְ (?) necklace [ham/mû/nā'k]

חֲבָל hurt, injury [hăbāl]

חֲלָק portion, lot [hălāq]

טְעַם*‡ (Pa) feed [ṭə'am"]

יְבַל*‡ (Ha) bring [yəbal"]

יְעַט advise; (ptc.) counselor; (Ithpa) deliberate [yə'aṭ]

כְּנַשׁ assemble [kənaš]

כָּרְסֵא seat, throne [kor/sē'']

לְבַשׁ‡ be clothed with [ləbaš]

לָהֵן‡ (I) (adv.) therefore [lā/hē'n]

לְחֵנָה* (pl.) concubine [ləhē/nā'"]

מְלַח‡ salt [məlaḥ]

מְנֵא mina (unit of weight) [mənē']

מַתְּנָה*‡ (pl.) gift [mat/tənâ"]

נְוָלוּ garbage heap; dung-hill [nəwā/lû']

נְצַל* (Ha) deliver, rescue [nəṣal"]

נְשָׂא‡ take, carry away [nəśā']

נִשְׁתְּוָן† decree [niš/təwā'n]

סוּמְפֹּנְיָה bagpipe? (musical instrument) [sûm/pō/nəyá']

עִיר§ watcher; (ext.) angel ['îr]

עִלָּה pretext ['il/lâ']

עֳפִי foliage, leaves ['ŏpî]

עִקַּר‡ root (stock) ['iq/qa'r]

עַתִּיק (adj.) old, aged ['at/tí'q]

צַוַּאר‡ neck [ṣaw/wa'r]

קְבַל*‡ (Pa) receive [qəbal"]

קַדְמָי first [qad/mā'i]

קְטַר* (pl.) knot, joint [qəṭar"]

קְצָת‡ end; part [qəṣāt]

רְגַשׁ*‡ (Ha) storm in? [rəḡaš"]

שְׂגָא§ grow, become great [śəḡā']

שָׂכְלְתָנוּ insight [śok/lətā/nú']

שְׂעַר hair [śə'ar]

שֵׁגָל* (pl.) concubine [šē/ḡā'l"]

שׁוּר*† (pl.) wall [šûr"]

שְׁחַת (ptc. pass.) corrupt; (n.) mischief [šəḥat]

שְׁלִם‡ (stat.) be finished [šəlim]

שֵׁן*† (d.) tooth [šēn"]

שְׁפַר‡ please, seem good [šəpar]

שֹׁרֶשׁ*‡ (pl.) root [šərōš"]

תַּלְתָּא triumvir? third part? [tal/tā']

תְּמַהּ* (pl.) wonder, miracle [təmah"]

K. Words Occurring 2 Times (88)

אֲדַרְגָּזַר* (pl. only) counselor [ʾădar/gā/zaʹrˣ]

אַזְדָּא (?) (adj. f.?) promulgated [ʾaz/dāʾ]

אֶלֶף‡ thousand [ʾălaʹp̄]

אֲנַף‡* (d.) face [ʾănap̄ˣ]

אֲפַרְסְכָי* (pl.; unc.) title of official? [ʾăpar/sekāʹiˣ]

אֹרַח‡* (pl.) way [ʾăraḥˣ]

אַרְכָה§ length(ening), prolongation [ʾar/kâ]

אִשֹּׁרֵן (?) timber? paneling? roof scaffolding? [ʾiš/rāʹn]

אֶשְׁתַּדּוּר revolt [ʾeš/tad/dúʹr]

בֵּין† (prep.) between [bên]

בָּעוּ petition, prayer [bā/ʿúʾ]

בַּת*† (pl.) bath (liquid measure) [batˣ]

גְּבוּרָה†† strength [gebú/ráʾ]

גְּדָבַר* (pl.) treasurer [gedā/barˣ]

גְּדַד‡ cut down [gedad]

גְּזֵרָה†† decree [gezē/ráʾ]

גְּלָל (coll.) blocks of stone [gelāl]

דִּבְרָה†† affair, matter [dib/raʾ]

דָּכְרוֹן* (pl.) minutes, memorandum [dok/rāʹnˣ]

דְּמָה‡ resemble [demâ]

דָּר§ generation [dār]

דֶּתֶא grass [deʹteʾ]

דְּתָבַר* (pl. n.) judge [detā/baʹrˣ]

הַדָּם* (pl.) member, limb [had/dāʹmˣ]

זוּעַ*‡ tremble [zúʹaˣ]

חֲזוֹת sight [ḥăzôt]

חֲמָה‡ rage, fury [ḥămâ]

חִנְטָה* (pl.) (grains of) wheat [ḥin/ṭâˣ]

חֲנַן‡† show mercy [ḥănan]

חֲסַן*‡ (Ha) take possession of, possess [ḥăsanˣ]

חֵסֶן might, wealth? [ḥēsēn]

חֲצַף* (Ha ptc. f.) harsh, severe [ḥăṣap̄ˣ]

טָב§ (adj.) good [ṭāb]

טוּר mountain [ṭûr]

טִין (wet) clay [ṭîn]

טְפַר* (pl.) (finger-) nail, claw [ṭeparˣ]

יְדָה*‡ (Ha) praise [yedâˣ]

יַם‡ sea [yam]

יַקִּיר (adj.) difficult; noble [yaq/qîʹr]

יְרַח‡ month [yeraḥ]

כְּתַל§ wall [ketal]

לְבוּשׁ†† garment [lebúš]

מֵאמַר‡ word, order [mēʾ/marˣ]

מָזוֹן food [mā/zóʹn]

מְלָא‡ fill [melāʾ]

מַלְאַךְ‡† angel [mal/ʾaʹk]

מַלְכָּה†† queen (-mother) [mal/kâʹ]

‡מִנְחָה offering [min/ḥấ]

מָרָד (adj.) rebellious [mā/rā́d]

מְשַׁח (anointing-) oil [məšaḥ]

נִבְזְבָּה present, gift [nəbiz/bá']

נִדְבָּךְ course (of stones, timber) [nid/bā́k]

נַהִירוּ illumination, insight [na!/hî/rú']

‡נְטַל lift up [nəṭal]

*נִיחֹחַ (pl.) incense [nî/ḥố'aḥ]

§*נְכַס (pl.) treasure, treasury; fine [nəkas]

נִפְקָה cost [nip̄/qá']

‡נְשַׁר eagle [nəšar]

‡סוּף be fulfilled; (Ha) annihilate [sûp̄]

*סַרְבָּל (pl.) trousers? tunic? cloak? [sar/bā́'l]

‡עוֹף bird; (coll.) birds ['ôp̄]

עִזְקָה signet-ring ['iz/qá']

פַּס hand [pas]

פְּרֵס half (-shekel); half (-mina)? [pərēs]

§פְּשַׁר interpret [pəšar]

פְּתַח (Pe pass.) open(ed) [pətaḥ]

פְּתָי width [pətāi]

‡צַד side [ṣad]

*צְלָה (Pa) pray [ṣəlá']

‡קַדְמָה former times [qad/mấ']

קְיָם statute, decree [qəyām]

קַיָּם (adj.) enduring [qay/yā́m]

*קְרַץ (pl.) piece; (in idiom.) slander [qəraṣ]

‡קְשֹׁט truth [qəšōṭ]

רִבּוֹ great number, ten thousand [rib/bố']

רֵו appearance [rêw]

§רְעוּ will, decision [rə'û]

‡רְעַע shatter [rə'a']

‡רְפַס trample down [rəpas]

‡שְׁבִיב flame [šəbîb]

‡שְׁוָה be like [šəwâ]

‡שְׁכַן live, dwell [šəkan]

‡שִׁלְטוֹן (pl.) high official [šil/ṭố'n]

שַׁפִּיר fair, lovely [šap/pî'r]

תְּדִיר duration [tədîr]

*תִּפְתָּי (pl.) police officer? magistrate? [tip̄/tā'i']

תְּקֵל shekel (unit of measure and weight) [təqēl]

תְּרַע door, opening; court [təra']

L. Words Occurring 1 Time (236)

*אִדְּר (pl.) threshing-floor ['id/da'r]

אַדְרַזְדָּא (adv.) diligently, zealously ['ad/raz/dā'']

אֶדְרָע	arm; (met) force [ʾed/rāʿ']
‡אַח*	(pl.) brother [ʾaḥ']
אֲחִידָה*	(pl.) riddle [ʾăḥi/dâ']
§אַחֲרִי	end [ʾaḥărî]
(?) אַחֲרִין	(adv.) at last [ʾa!/ḥări'n]
אֵימְתָן	(adj.) frightful [ʾê/mətā'n]
‡אֲנַס	(ptc.) distress [ʾănas]
אַנְתּוּן	(pers. pron., m. pl.) you [ʾan/tú'n]
אֲפַרְסָי*	(pl.; unc.) gent? title of official? [ʾăpā/rəsā'i']
אֲפַרְסַתְכָי*	(pl.) title of officials [ʾăpar/sat/kā'i']
אַפְּתֹם	treasury? [ʾap/pətō'm]
אֲרִיךְ	fitting [ʾărîk]
אַרְכֻּבָּה*	(pl.) knee [ʾar/kub/bâ']
אַרְעִי	bottom [ʾar/ʿî']
אֲרַק	earth [ʾăraq]
אֶשָּׁא	fire [ʾeš/šā']
בְּאִישׁ*	(f. def.) evil, bad [bə'îš']
‡בְּאֵשׁ	(stat.) be bad [bə'ēš]
בַּדַּר*	(Pa) scatter [badar']
בְּהִילוּ	hurry, haste [bəhi/lû']
בִּינָה†	insight, discernment [bî/nâ']
בִּירָה	citadel, fortress [bî/rá']
בִּית*	pass the night [bît']
בָּל	heart; (ext.) mind [bāl]
‡בְּלָה*	(Pa) wear (someone) down [bəlâ']
בִּנְיָן†	building [bin/yā'n]
בְּנַס	become angry [bənas]
בִּקְעָה†	plain [biq/ʿâ']
(I) ‡בְּרַךְ	kneel down [bərak]
‡בְּרַךְ*	(pl.) knee [bərak']
גַּב*	(pl.) back? side? [gab']
§גִּבָּר*	(pl.) strong man [gib/ba'r']
גֵּוָה†	pride [gē/wâ']
§גּוּחַ*	(Ha) stir up [gú'aḥ']
גִּזְבָּר*	(pl.) treasurer [giz/ba'r']
§גִּיר	(n.) plaster [gîr]
גַּלְגַּל*†	(pl.) wheel [gal/ga'l']
‡גְּמַר	(ptc. pass.) finished [gəmar]
‡גֶּרֶם*	(pl.) bone [gəram']
דֹּב†	bear [dōb]
דְּבַח	(v.) sacrifice [dəbaḥ]
דְּבַח*	(pl. n.) sacrifice [dəbaḥ']
‡דְּבַק	stick (hold) together [dəbaq]
(?) דְּהוּא	(corr.?) that is [dəhú']
‡דּוּשׁ*	trample down [dúš']
דַּחֲוָה*	(pl.) food? diversion? [da!/ḥăwâ']
דִּין†	(v.) judge [dîn']
דַּיָּן*†	(pl. n.) judge [day/yā'n']
דִּינָיֵא	judges [di/nā/yē']
דִּכְרוֹן	minutes, memorandum [dik/ró'n]
‡דְּלַק	burn [dəlaq]

דְּרָע* (pl.) arm [dərā'ᵉ]

הָא ‡ (interj.) behold! [hā']

הֵא(־כְדִי)† just as [hē'(-kədi)]

הַרְהֹר* (pl.) dream-fantasies [har/hō'r]

זְבַן buy [zəban]

זְהִיר* (pl. adj.) cautious, careful [zəhîr]

זוּד*‡ (Ha) act insolently [zûd]

זוּן* (Hith) feed on, live on [zûn]

זָכוּ § innocence [zā/kú']

זְמַן*‡ (Hith) agree [zəman]

זַמָּר* (pl.) singer [zam/mā'r]

זְעֵיר (adj.) small [zə'êr]

זְעִק‡ cry out, shout [zə'iq]

זְקַף‡ (ptc. pass.) impaled [zəqap̄]

זְרַע‡ (coll.) seed; (ext.) descendants [zəra']

חֲבוּלָה crime [ḥăbû/lá']

חֲדֶה* (pl.) breast [ḥădēh]

חֶדְוָה† joy [ḥed/wâ']

חֲדַת new [ḥădat]

חוּט (?) * repair? inspect? [ḥûṭ]

חִוָּר white [ḥiw/wā'r]

חֲטָי § sin [ḥăṭāi]

חַטָּיָה § (K) sin-offering [ḥaṭ/ṭā/yâ']

חַסִּיר § (adj.) defective, of poor quality [ḥas/sí'r]

חֲרַב* (Ho) be devastated, destroyed [ḥărab]

חֲרַךְ* (Hithpa) be singed (by fire) [ḥărak]

חֲרַץ § hip [ḥăraṣ]

חֲשַׁב‡ reckon, regard [ḥăšab]

חֲשׁוֹךְ § darkness [ḥăšôk]

חֲשַׁח (v.) need [ḥăšaḥ]

חַשְׁחָה* (pl. n.) need [ḥaš/ḥā']

חַשְׁחוּ (n.) need [ḥaš/ḥû']

חֲשַׁל crush, pulverize [ḥăšal]

חֲתַם‡ (v.) seal [ḥătam]

טָאֵב (stat.) be good [ṭə'êb]

טַבָּח*† (pl.) executioner, bodyguard [ṭab/bā'ḥ]

טְוָת (n.) fasting; (adv.) in fasting [ṭəwāt]

טְלַל*§ (Ha) make a nest [ṭəlal]

טַרְפְּלָיֵ* (pl.) class of officials? [ṭar/pəlā'i]

יַבֶּשָׁה‡ dry land; (def.) the earth [yab/bəšá']

יְגַר heap of stones [yəgar]

יְטַב‡ it suits, pleases [yəṭab]

יְסַף*‡ (Ho) be added [yəsap̄]

יְצָא* (Sha) finish [yəṣā']

יְצַב*‡ (Pa) make certain (of) [yəṣab]

יְקֵדָה burning [yəqē/dá']

יַרְכָה* (pl.) upper thigh [yar/ká']

יָת accusative particle; object marker (not translated) [yāt]

כִּדְבָה a lie (falsehood) [kid/bá']

‡כָּה	(adv.) here, hitherto [kâ]
כַּוָּה*	(pl.) window [kaw/wâ"]
‡כַּכַּר*	(pl.) talent (weight) [kak/ka'r"]
כֹּר, כּוֹר*	(pl.) kor (dry measure) [kōr", kôr"]
כַּרְבְּלָה*	(pl.) cap [kar/bəlâ"]
כְּרָה*	(Ith) be anxious [kərâ"]
כָּרוֹז	herald [kā/rô'z]
כְּרִז*	(Ha) proclaim [kəraz"]
לְוָת*	(prep.) near, beside [ləwāt"]
‡לְחֶם	bread; (ext.) meal, feast [laḥem]
§מֹאזְנֵא	balance (scales) [mō'/zənē']
מְגִלָּה†‡	scroll [məḡil/lá']
‡מְגַר*	(Pa) overthrow [məḡar"]
מַדְבַּח	altar [mad/ba'ḥ]
‡מוֹת	death [môt]
§מַחְלְקָה*	(pl.) division (of Levites) [maḥ/ləqâ"]
מְלַח	eat (the) salt; (idiom.) be under obligation of loyalty [məlaḥ]
מְלַךְ	(n.) counsel [məlak]
מִנְיָן	(n.) number [min/yā'n]
מַעְבָד*†	(pl.) work [ma!/'ăbād"]
§מְעֵה*	(pl.) belly [mə'ēh"]
מֶעָל*	(pl.) sunset [me!/'ā'l"]
‡מְרַד	rebellion [mərad]
‡מְרַט (?)	(stat.) be plucked out [məriṭ]
‡מִשְׁכַּן	dwelling, abode [miš/ka'n]
‡מִשְׁתֵּא	(drinking-) feast [miš/tē']
‡נְבָא*	(Hithpa) prophesy [nəbā'"]
‡נְבוּאָה	prophecy, prophesying [nəbû/'á']
נֶבְרְשָׁה	lampstand [neb/rəšá']
‡נְגַד	(v.) flow [nəḡad]
נֶגֶד†	(prep.) toward [ne'/ḡed]
נְגַהּ	brightness [nəḡah]
‡נְדַד	flee [nədad]
נִדְנֶה	(n.) sheath? body?; (ext.) on account of this [nid/ne'h]
נְהוֹר; נְהִיר	(Q; K) light [nəhôr; nahîr]
נוּד*	flee [nûd"]
נְטַר	keep (in one's heart) [nəṭar]
‡נְמַר	panther [nəmar]
‡נְסַח*	(Hith) be pulled out [nəsaḥ"]
‡נְסַךְ*	(Pa) offer [nəsak"]
נְסַךְ*	(pl.) drink-offering, libation [nəsak"]
נִצְבָּה	firmness, hardness [niṣ/bá']
‡נְצַח*	(Hithpa) distinguish oneself [nəṣaḥ"]

§נְקֵא	(adj.) pure [nəqē']	עֲצִיב	(adj.) sorrowful, afflicted ['ăṣîb]
‡נְקַשׁ	knock together [nəqaš]		
*נְשִׁין	(pl.) wife [nəšîn"]	‡*עֲקַר	(Ith) be plucked out ['ăqar"]
‡נִשְׁמָה	breath [niš/mấ']	‡עָר	adversary ['ār]
†נְתִין	(pl.) (temple-) slave [nətîn"]	§*עֲרָד	(pl.) wild ass, onager? ['ărād"]
*נְתַר	(A) shake off [nətar"]	‡עַרְוָה	dishonor ['ar/wấ']
‡*סְבַל	(Po ptc.) be preserved? erect? [səbal"]	‡עֲשַׁת	think, plan ['ăšat]
§סְבַר	seek, strive [səbar]	‡*עֲתִיד	(pl. adj.) ready to ['ătîd"]
סְגַר	shut [səḡar]	פֶּחָר	potter [pe!/ḥā'r]
‡*סְעַד	(Pa) support [sə'ad"]	*פַּטִּישׁ	(pl.) garment (coat? trousers?) [paṭ/ṭǐ'š"]
(I) ‡*סְתַר	(Pa ptc. pass.) hidden things [sətar"]	‡פְּלַג	(v.) divide [pəlaḡ]
(II) §סְתַר	destroy, demolish [sətar]	‡פְּלַג	(n.) half [pəlaḡ]
†עוֹד	(adv.) still, yet ['ôd]	*פְּלֻגָּה	(pl.) division (of priests) [pəlug/gấ"]
*עֲוָיָה	(pl.) offense ['ăwā/yá"]	פֻּלְחָן	(cultic) service [pol/ḥā'n]
עוּר	chaff ['úr]		
*עֵז	(pl.) goat ['ēz"]	‡פְּרַס	divide [pəras]
עֵטָה	counsel ['ē/ṭá']	‡פְּרַק	unloose, abolish [pəraq]
עֵלָּה	above ['ē'l/lâ]	‡*פְּרַשׁ	(Pa ptc. pass.) separate(ly)? [pəraš"]
(?)*עֲלָוָה	(pl.) burnt offering ['al/wấ"]	צְבוּ	thing, matter [ṣəbû]
†עִלִּי	roof chamber ['il/lî']	צְדָא	(interr.) is it true? [ṣədā']
*עֲלַע	(pl.) rib ['ăla'"]	‡צִדְקָה	beneficence, justice [ṣid/qấ']
*עַמִּיק	(pl. adj.) deep, impenetrable (things) ['am/mǐq"]	‡*צְפִיר	(pl.) he-goat [ṣəpîr"]
עֲמַר	wool ['ămar]	קֵיט	summer [qa'/yiṭ]
*עֲנֵה	(pl. adj.) miserable ['ănēh"]	‡קְנָה	buy [qənâ]
‡*עֲנָן	(pl.) clouds ['ănān"]	‡קְצַף	become furious [qəṣap]
עֲנַשׁ	fine (imposed) ['ănāš]		

קְצַף‡ (n) wrath [qəṣap̄]

קְצַץ‡* (Pa) cut off [qəṣaṣ*]

קְרָב†‡ war [qərāb]

רְגַז* (Ha) anger, enrage [rəḡaz*]

רְגַז‡ (n.) rage [rəḡaz]

רַחִיק* (pl. adj.) far [ra!/ḥî'q*]

רַחֲמִין§ compassion [ra!/ḥămî'n]

רְחַץ* (Hith) rely (on) [rəḥaṣ*]

רֵיחַ (n.) smell [rê'aḥ]

רַעֲנַן‡ (adj.) prosperous, flourishing [ra!/'ănan]

שָׂהֲדוּ testimony [śā/ḥădû']

שְׂטַר side [śəṭar]

שְׂכַל‡* (Hith) consider [śəkal*]

שְׂנֵא (ptc.) adversary [śənē']

שְׁאֵלָה† question [šə'ē/lá']

שְׁבַט‡* (pl.) tribe [šəbaṭ*]

שְׁבַשׁ* (Hithpa) be perplexed [šəbaš*]

שְׁדַר* (Hithpa) be like [šədar*]

שֵׁיצִיא (loanword; v.) finish [šê/ṣí']

שְׁלֵה§ (adj.) at ease [šəlēh]

שְׁלֵוָה‡ prosperity, fortune [šəlē/wâ']

שְׁמַד‡* (Ha) destroy, exterminate [šəmad*]

שְׁמַם‡* (Ithpo) stiffen with fright [šəmam*]

שְׁמַשׁ* (Pa) serve [šəmaš*]

שְׁמַשׁ‡ sun [šəmaš]

שְׁנָה‡ (II) (n.) sleep [šənâ]

שְׁפַט‡ (ptc.) judge [šəp̄aṭ]

שְׁפַל‡ low(ly) [šəp̄al]

שְׁפַרְפָּר dawn [šəp̄ar/pā'r]

שָׁק§* (d.) (lower) leg [šāq*]

שֵׁרֹשׁוּ (?) banishment, exclusion [šərō/šú']

תְּבַר break [təbar]

תְּוַהּ be alarmed [təwah]

תְּלַג snow [təlaḡ]

תְּלִיתָי third [təlî/tā'i]

תִּנְיָן second [tin/yā'n]

תִּנְיָנוּת (adv.) a second time [tin/yā/nú't]

תְּקַל weigh [təqal]

תְּקַן‡* (Ho) be reestablished [təqan*]

תְּקָף strength [təqāp̄]

תְּקֹף strength [təqōp̄]

תָּרָע* (pl.) doorkeeper [tā/rā'*]

INDEX TO HEBREW VOCABULARY

Hebrew and Aramaic words are indexed separately. Verbs are given no vowel points. Other words are also unpointed, except for forms with identical consonantal spelling. Root numbers in parentheses differentiate between identical spellings with different meanings. References are to Section number (1–6), and Subsection letter (A–Z, AA, BB). For convenience the number of occurrences is also given for Hebrew and Aramaic words.

INDEX TO ARAMAIC VOCABULARY